I0481295

CROSS-CULTURAL BUSINESS LEADERSHIP
IN THAILAND

Insights from 178 Expatriate Senior Managers

CHIN-JU TSAI, PH. D.

Your essential guide to working with the Thais

ISBN-13: 978-1981737727

For his love, support and belief in me,
this book is dedicated to my father, Hai-Ching Tsai.

Contents

Acknowledgments

Executive Summary

About the Author

ACKNOWLEDGEMENTS

I would like to thank the 178 expatriates who shared their views and experiences linked to managing and leading Thai employees. Reading and analysing their responses to the interview and survey questions was a journey that was both enjoyable and inspiring. Their dedications to helping their companies achieve their organisational goals through leading people, their cultural learning and adjustment journey, their strategic consideration for managing people and the sense of achievement as well as that of frustration they experienced in the process are vividly presented in their words. Their participation in the research has made it possible to help both academics and practitioners understand cross-cultural leadership adjustment issues, particularly in the context of Thailand and anywhere leaders face a high degree of novelty in terms of their subordinates' characteristics.

Here is a list of 19 expatriates who consented to have their names shown in the book: Christian Baillet, Richard Belair, Frédéric Borgoltz, Stephane Debeusscher, Remko Vleesch Dubois, Marcel Ewals, Emmanuel Fauvel, Paul Gambles, Daniel Giles, Mario Hardy, Hannu Helo, David Hoard, David Lawrence, Fred May, Tom Racette, Rehan Saghir, James Seymour, Itty Varugis and Anthony Watanabe. This book could not have been written without each of them and the other 159 anonymous expatriates.

I would also like to thank Professor Chris Carr of the University of Edinburgh for his support during the research project and Ms. Sasiya Supprakit for conducting and transcribing the interviews.

EXECUTIVE SUMMARY

This book is based on the views and experiences of 178 expatriate senior managers and was written for the benefit of expatriate business managers and anyone interested in gaining insights into cross-cultural leadership in Thailand. The book intends to help readers understand: 1) the unique values, attitudes, behaviours, needs, and expectations of Thai employees, 2) how their work attitudes and behaviours are influenced by tradition, religion and social customs, 3) the modes/patterns by which expatriate leaders adjust, and 4) ways to effectively manage and lead Thai employees.

In the book, it is revealed that many of the expatriate managers considered leading/managing employees in Thailand to be very different from what it had been in the other countries they had worked in, and that Thailand is one of the most challenging places in which to lead. This is because Thai employees possess an array of unique characteristics; their cultural values and beliefs and their work behaviours differ significantly from those found in the expatriates' home and other countries. When faced with such unique employee characteristics and different work values and behaviours, the expatriate business leaders reacted in a number of different ways. Some adjusted their own approaches, others tried to change those of their staff, and still others did both. The challenges they faced and their suggestions on how to overcome them are illustrated in this book.

The key aspects presented in this book are summarised below:

I. The expatriate leaders' views on the characteristics of their Thai employees

A number of unique characteristics of Thai employees were mentioned by the expatriates; these had a great influence on the way they led/managed them. The five most mentioned characteristics are 1) Thai employees tend not to speak up, particularly in meetings; 2) they hold a high degree of respect for seniority and hierarchy; 3) most of them would go to any length to avoid losing face; 4) they show little initiative and expect to be given detailed instructions; and 5) they are mild-mannered and non-confrontational.

II. The expatriate leaders' modes of cross-cultural leadership adjustment (CLA)

Most expatriate business leaders simultaneously adjusted their leadership approaches and tried to change their Thai employees in order to meet local conditions and to match their personal requirements. Only a small proportion either only modified their leadership approaches or tried to change their subordinates.

III. The challenges faced by the expatriate leaders in managing Thai employees

The challenges found in leading Thai employees were mainly associated with their characteristics. The key challenges are: 1) communication and language barriers; 2) the short supply of talent and the high employee turnover; 3) the low employee sense of ownership and accountability; 4) the need to adjust one's own leadership approach and learn to work within local cultural and societal expectations; and 5) the high resistance to change of Thai employees.

IV. The expatriate leaders' suggestions for leading Thai employees.

Several suggestions for effectively leading Thai employees were provided by the expatriates. The key suggestions are: 1) learn and respect the local culture; 2) use indirect approaches; 3) be patient; 4) give clear instructions and monitor progress; 5) avoid Thai staff losing face; 6) build trusting relationships; 7) overcome language barriers; 8) spend more time on coaching and development; 9) encourage staff to take initiatives and responsibilities; and 10) build a working environment that is fun and allows open communication.

In this book, many direct quotes from the expatriates' responses are used. It is hoped that the use of the expatriates' own words will make the book interesting to read and enable readers to formulate their own interpretations and judgements.

ABOUT THE AUTHOR

Chin-Ju Tsai, MA, PhD., is Senior Lecturer (Associate Professor) of Human Resource Management at Royal Holloway, University of London. Prior to this, she held a research position at Warwick Business School, University of Warwick, and a management position at Standard Chartered Bank. She holds a PhD in Management Studies from the University of Cambridge. She is a Member of the Academy of Management (AoM) and a Fellow of the Higher Education Academy (FHEA). Her research focusses on cross-cultural leadership, international human resource management, strategic human resource management, organizational performance, workplace emotion, human resource development, and employment relations in SMEs. Her work has appeared in top management journals including *Human Relations, Human Resource Management Journal, Work and Occupations, International Journal of Human Resource Management, Organization,* and *International Small Business Journal.* She was the winner of the Academy of Management (AoM) annual conference's Best Paper (HR Division) award 2017, the International Academy of Management and Business (IAMB) conference's Best Overall Paper award 2015, and of the *International Small Business Journal*'s Best Overall Paper award 2010.

PART I.
CROSS-CULTURAL BUSINESS LEADERSHIP AND ADJUSTMENT

CHAPTER 1. INTRODUCTION

This book is based on the views and experiences of 178 expatriate senior managers and was written for the benefit of expatriate business managers who are currently working or plan to work in Thailand. It can also provide good reference to researchers and management consultants who wish to gain empirical insights into cross-cultural leadership in Thailand and to general readers wishing to understand the management issues encountered in Thai workplaces.

The rapid growth of the international business market makes effective cross-border management and leading of employees an important item on the agenda of business managers and multinational corporations. However, cross-cultural management can be challenging for many expatriate managers, as some of their approaches may not always be compatible with the host countries' cultures.

Leadership theories, such as the *Situational leadership theory* proposed by Hersey and Blanchard (Hersey & Blanchard, 1982) and the *Culturally endorsed implicit theories of leadership* developed by Robert House and his colleagues (R. J. House, P. J. Hanges, M. Javidan, P. W. Dorfman, & V. Gupta, 2004), argue that the adjustment of leadership behaviours is crucial to leadership effectiveness. However, researchers have not given leadership adjustment in a cross-cultural context the attention it deserves; virtually no *empirical* research has studied the adjustments involved in cross-cultural leadership. Thus, we hitherto had no knowledge of whether expatriate leaders, when leading cross-culturally, adjust their leadership approaches to address local employee characteristics or whether they attempt to change local employee attitudes to meet their requirements. We also had no information on the patterns by which expatriate managers adjust.

To fill the aforementioned knowledge gaps, I conducted a research project in Thailand. My research was aimed at providing answers to the following questions:
- How do expatriate senior managers lead/manage their Thai employees?

1

- Do they adjust their leadership approaches to cater for the characteristics of Thai employees and local work practices? And, if so, how do they adjust them? What factors influence their adjustment, and why?
- Do they try to change the ways in which Thai employees work? And, if so, what do they try to change and why?
- What are their patterns of adjustment?
- Do they encounter any challenges when managing/ leading Thai employees?
- What are their suggestions for leading Thai employees?

In this book, I present my findings on the following key aspects:

- The expatriate senior managers' views on the characteristics of their Thai employees.
- The expatriate senior managers' modes/patterns of cross-cultural leadership adjustment (CLA).
- The challenges faced by the expatriate senior managers in managing their Thai employees.
- The expatriate senior managers' suggestions for managing Thai employees

In presenting my findings, I often use the very words spoken by the expatriates' to illustrate their views and experiences. I do so in the hope that this will 1) make the book interesting to read; 2) help readers understand and see for themselves the reasons why the expatriate leaders held their particular views or perspectives, behaved in the way they did, and used particular approaches; and 3) enable readers to formulate their own interpretations and judgements.

Thailand is often called the "land of smiles" because of its friendly people, rich history, unique culture and natural beauty. It is also the home of traditional, religious, and social customs that differ significantly from those of other countries. If you were an expatriate who had led/managed employees in your or other countries, you would find Thailand to be a most challenging place in which to lead. This is because Thai employees possess an array of unique characteristics that differ substantially from those found in your home country and in other countries in which you may have worked. For example—as observed by the expatriate business leaders who participated in my research—Thai employees tend not to speak up, particularly in meetings; they perceive any negative feedback on the work they performed as personal criticisms; they go to almost any length to save 'face'; they assign great importance to social and fun elements in the workplace; etc. Many of the expatriates stated that unmodified western methods rarely work in Thailand and that it had taken time for them to adjust to the Thai ways of doing things.

I believe that the expatriates' experiences presented here will provide others with in-depth insights for leading/managing Thai employees that will prove more useful than those reported by Thai leaders, as the Thai employees' work behaviours change when they are being supervised by non-Thai managers.

I hope that this book will help expatriate managers understand: 1) the unique values, attitudes, behaviours, needs, and expectations of Thai employees; 2) how their work attitudes and behaviours are influenced by traditional, religious, and social customs; and 3) how to respond to the Thai employees' unique work attitudes and behaviours, behave in acceptable ways, and avoid misunderstandings. I also hope that this book will help expatriate managers make sense of their own and other leaders' approaches, adjust to the lovely and polite Thai society, and come up with even more effective ways by which to lead/manage Thai employees.

The remainder of the book is structured as follows:
Chapter 2 describes the concept of leadership adjustment and briefly summarize two relevant leadership theories in order to underline the importance of CLA.
Chapter 3 explains how the research was conducted.
Chapter 4 presents Thailand's historical, political, and economic background.
Chapter 5 provides a review of the literature on Thailand's cultural values.
Chapter 6 presents five main characteristics of Thai employees, as perceived by the expatriate senior managers, to show how these had influenced the expatriates' leadership approaches.
Chapter 7 reports the expatriates' modes/patterns of adjustment.
Chapter 8 details the challenges faced by the expatriates when leading Thai employees.
Chapter 9 provides the expatriates' suggestions for leading/managing Thai employees.
Chapter 10 concludes with my views on the issue of the fit between leadership approaches, employee characteristics and cultural norms.

CHAPTER 2. LEADERSHIP AND CROSS-CULTURAL LEADERSHIP ADJUSTMENT

LEADERSHIP

Leadership has been a notable research topic for at least the past few decades, yet academic researchers and practitioners still have no consensus on its definition (Hollander & Offermann, 1990; Morrison & Von Glinow, 1990). Leadership has been defined based on various aspects. Simonton (1994: 411) defines a leader as a 'group member whose influence on group attitudes, performance, or decision making greatly exceeds that of the average member of the group'. G. Yukl (1998: 5) defines leadership as 'a specialized role and a social influence process'. Stogdill (1950) considers it 'the process of influencing activities of an organized group in its efforts toward goal setting and goal achievement' (cited in Bass & Stogdill, 1990: 13). In addition, House, Javidan, Hanges, and Dorfman (2002: 5) define leadership in the organizational context as 'the ability of an individual to influence, motivate, and enable others to contribute toward the effectiveness and success of the organizations of which they are members'.

Although the definitions of leadership vary in their details, they share some commonalities. For example, leadership is seen as having an influence or creating an impact on other members of the group to achieve certain goals; leadership does not exist without influence (P. G. Northouse, 2006); it is regarded as a group phenomenon; and there can be no leaders without followers (Nahavandi, 2006).

LEADERSHIP THEORIES RELATED TO LEADERSHIP ADJUSTMENT

Several leadership theories have been developed over the past few decades, including trait theories, style and behavioural theories, situational and contingency theories, leader-member exchange theories and the new leadership theories (transformational, visionary and charismatic). Here, I provide a brief review of two theories that are relevant to leadership adjustment: situational leadership theories and the culturally endorsed implicit theories of leadership.

Situational Leadership Theories Situational theories emerged as a result of the shortcomings associated with trait theories and behavioural theories; namely, trait and behavioural theories ignore the situational factors that are tied to leadership (Hollander & Offermann, 1990). Many scholars (e.g. Fiedler, 1967; Hemphill, 1949; House, 1971; Mullins, 1999; Vroom & Yetton, 1974) propose that the qualities demanded of leaders depend on situations, and the required qualities may vary. Building on Reddin (1967) 3D management style theory, Hersey and Blanchard (1972 and 1982) developed situational leadership theory (SLT). The central proposition of this theory is that leaders should modify their leadership style according to the task-relevant maturity of their followers. It proposes that an optimal leadership style (defined as specific combinations of leader task and relationship behaviours) should match the levels of subordinate maturity (defined as a combination of follower commitment and competence). For example, with subordinates of very low-level maturity, managers are advised to adopt a 'telling' style; on the other hand, with subordinates of very high maturity, a 'delegating' style is recommended.

SLT is among the most known leadership theories, and has been covered in many textbooks and used in leadership training programmes. However, the theory has been criticized as being prescriptive and lacking empirical support (Graeff, 1983; P. G. Northouse, 2007; Thompson & Vecchio, 2009; Vecchio, 1987; G. Yukl, 2006). Although the validity of SLT is yet to be verified, its main contributions include highlighting the importance of flexibility in leadership behaviour, and considering the degree of maturity of subordinates as an important situational determinant of appropriate leader behaviour (Graeff, 1983; P. G. Northouse, 2007).

Culturally Endorsed Implicit Theories of Leadership (CLTs). While SLT draws our attention to consider the characteristics of followers, the culturally endorsed implicit theories of leadership (referred to as CLTs in House et al., 2004) go a step further and consider leadership in intercultural settings. CLTs were developed based on implicit leadership theory (ILT), which contends that individuals hold a set of beliefs regarding the kinds of traits, characteristics, skills, and behaviours that constitute effective or ineffective leadership, and that such beliefs influence the extent to which individuals accept others as their leaders (Robert G. Lord,

Binning, Rush, & Thomas, 1978; Robert G. Lord, De Vader, & Alliger, 1986; Robert G. Lord, Foti, & De Vader, 1984; R. G. Lord & Maher, 1991).

Extending ILT to the cross-cultural context, House and his colleagues proposed CLTs and argued that beliefs about leadership are shared among individuals from the same cultural background, and that expectations regarding the best way to lead are culturally endorsed (see Den Hartog, House, Hanges, Ruiz-Quintanilla, & Dorfman, 1999; House & Aditya, 1997; R. J. House, P. J. Hanges, M. Javidan, P. Dorfman, & V. Gupta, 2004; Javidan, Dorfman, De Luque, & House, 2006); therefore, 'expected, accepted, and effective leader behaviour varies by cultures' (House & Aditya, 1997: 454).

The CLTs' assertion that variation in what is expected of a leader exists among different cultures has received support from several empirical studies. For example, it had been found that, in high power distance cultures such as those of China, Taiwan, Mexico, and Venezuela, subordinates expect their leaders to wield greater authority and prefer paternalistic leadership styles that combine autocratic decisions with supportive behaviours (Adsit, London, Crom, & Jones, 1997; Dickson, Den Hartog, & Mitchelson, 2003; Dorfman, et al., 1997). In contrast, in low power distance cultures such as those of Western Europe, New Zealand, and the United States, participative leadership is seen as a more favourable attribute (Dorfman, Hanges, & Brodbeck, 2004).

Evidence from GLOBE research (House et al, 2004) showed that people from similar cultures agree in their beliefs about leadership. Thus, it is suggested that, to be effective and accepted by followers, leaders need to adjust their behaviours in order to meet their followers' cultural expectations. House et al., (2004) also suggested that the greater the cultural differences are between expatriate managers and local employees, the greater is the need for mutual adjustment.

CROSS-CULTURAL LEADERSHIP ADJUSTMENT (CLA)

Although both SLT and CLTs emphasize the importance of adjusting leadership approaches to address the characteristics of followers, empirical research examining whether leaders do so and the ways in which they do so, particularly in a cross-cultural setting, is virtually non-existent.

Adjustment in a cross-cultural setting is commonly regarded as the process by which an individual achieves a 'fit and reduced conflict between the environmental demands and the individual's behavioral and attitudinal inclinations' (Zimmermann & Sparrow, 2007: 66). This broad definition is derived from expatriate adjustment research, which mainly focusses on the *degree* to which expatriate managers adjust to their host countries in three dimensions: general, social interaction, and work/role adjustment (Black, 1988; Black & Stephens, 1989; Peltokorpi & Froese, 2012; Ravasi, Salamin, & Davoine, 2015; Shaffer, Harrison, & Gilley, 1999). These three dimensions are mainly based on the work of Black and colleagues (see, e.g., Black, Mendenhall, & Oddou, 1991; Black & Stephens, 1989) and have been used as a theoretical underpinning by numerous studies (see, e.g., Black, 1988; Black & Stephens, 1989; Peltokorpi & Froese, 2012; Ravasi, et al., 2015; Shaffer, et al., 1999). Although the dimension of work/role adjustment has been examined, no detailed account has been provided for the *modes/patterns* through which expatriate leaders adjust their *leadership role*.

In cross-cultural leadership research, I found that most studies have examined how the leaders' own cultural values influence their leadership styles (see e.g. Brodbeck, et al., 2000; Brodbeck, Frese, & Javidan, 2002; Javidan & Carl, 2005; K. Lee, Scandura, & Sharif, 2014; Leung & Bozionelos, 2004); only a small number of studies have examined how expatriate managers react to new cultures and why and how they adjust their leadership styles. Festing and Maletzky (2011) defined CLA as 'the process of synchronization of incompatible work-related interaction routines' (p. 186) and argued that, to be successful in foreign assignments, expatriate leaders need to find a way of bringing together apparently incompatible routines (e.g. work patterns, leadership approaches) between expatriates and local employees. The focus is on the fit between leadership approaches and follower characteristics, as the leading and management of subordinates is central to the leadership role. Consistent with this argument, my study sees CLA as the process by which expatriate business leaders adjust their leadership approaches and/or change their subordinates to balance conflicting demands in cross-cultural contexts.

Overall, CLA has not received enough attention from researchers. As pointed out by Festing and Maletzky (2011), leadership adjustment has been neglected in the extant research on expatriate adjustment and the 'results of current conceptual and empirical research do not allow one to draw adequate conclusions regarding the adjustment of leadership behavior' (p.190). My research set out to fill this void by exploring the CLA modes of expatriate senior business leaders working in a cultural setting different from that of their home countries. The next chapter presents how the research was conducted.

7

Chapter Two Executive Summary
Leadership and Cross-cultural Leadership Adjustment

- The definitions of leadership vary; it has been defined based on various perspectives. The various definitions have in common that leadership is seen as having an influence or creating an impact on other members of a group towards the achievement of certain goals. Leadership does not exist without influence; it is regarded as a group phenomenon and there can be no leaders without followers.

- Both situational leadership theory (SLT) and the culturally endorsed implicit theories of leadership (CLTs) emphasize the importance of adjusting leadership approaches to address the characteristics of followers.

- Cross-cultural leadership adjustment (CLA) has not received enough attention from researchers, empirical research examining whether leaders adjust their leadership approaches and the ways in which they do so, particularly in a cross-cultural setting, is virtually non-existent.

- My research explores the CLA modes/patterns of expatriate senior business leaders working in a cultural setting different from that of their home countries. CLA is seen as the process by which expatriate business leaders adjust their leadership approaches and/or change their subordinates to balance conflicting demands in cross-cultural contexts.

CHAPTER 3. THE STUDY METHODOLOGY

This book is based on data and information collected from 178 expatriate business leaders working in Thailand through two methods: 1) semi-structured interviews with 13 expatriate executives; and 2) a qualitative on-line survey of 165 expatriate senior managers.

Interview
The interviews were carried out with four American, five British and four Japanese CEOs working in Bangkok. The format of the interviews was individual, face-to-face semi-structured which allowed flexibility and maximum exploration of the research issues. In the interviews, the expatriates were asked about their views on the characteristics of Thai employees, business systems and culture, their leadership approaches, and whether or not the host culture, employees and environment influenced their leadership approaches. They were also asked whether they needed to adjust their leadership approaches and/or change Thai employees and work practices. Also, if they reported having needed to adjust, they were asked what had led to that need and what they had done to address it. From the interviews, we learned the importance of the characteristics of Thai employees, local culture and business practices, and of the leaders' perspectives in influencing leadership adjustment. The findings of the interviews were used as the basis upon which to develop the subsequent on-line survey.

Online Survey

The expatriates who completed the on-line survey were contacted through LinkedIn. I used it to compile the sampling frame as a compiled contact list of expatriate senior managers was not readily available. LinkedIn is the largest business-oriented professional networking platform on the Internet, with over 313 million users in more than 200 countries as of October 2014 (LindedIn, 2014). LinkedIn allows users to create professional profiles; through these, I was able to view the people's work information (e.g. occupation, job role, job level, work experience, country where they worked, industry sector, year of service) and to select research samples.

Two sampling criteria were used. A) the job levels had to be senior, with job titles such as CEO, CFO, director, chairman, managing director, president, senior vice president and general manager. I selected senior managers as my research respondents because they are commonly regarded as leadership figures and are critically important to the success of their organizations; thus, the results obtained from the study of their experiences can greatly contribute to our understanding of leadership and of organizational practices. B) the sample selected was not to comprise Thai nationals; this was effected by checking the names and photos shown on LinkedIn profiles.

The survey consisted of three sets of open-ended questions designed to gain insights into the expatriate leaders' viewpoints, experiences and insights that could not otherwise have been extracted from responses to close-ended questions. The questions are presented in the Appendix. The first set of questions was designed to explore the expatriate leaders' approaches in leading Thai subordinates and to investigate whether local employees, culture and business practices had influenced their approaches. The second was designed to investigate whether the expatriates had adjusted their leadership approaches, and the third explored whether they had changed (or had tried to change) their subordinates and/or the subsidiaries' work practices. The respondents' answers to the questions provided rich information on their views on local situations and on their adjustment behaviors. An additional and final set of questions asked the respondents to provide demographic information. The survey was administered through Qualtrics, an online survey platform, and ran from October 2014 to February 2015.

Table 1 presents the profiles of the participants. The majority were male (94.9%), which replicated the low ratio of females holding senior positions reported in the business press (Fairchild, 2014; Morris, 2013). Over three-quarters (75.9%) were aged between 40 and 59 years old. The sample group covered 25 different nationalities and over 30 industries. About two-thirds (67.4%) of the respondents had worked more than 5 years in Thailand, with 24.1% having worked there more than 15 years.

10

Table1. Profile of the 178 expatriate business leaders

	Interview (13 expats)		On-line survey (165 expats.)		All participants (178 expats.)	
	No. of expatriates	(%)	No. of expatriates	(%)	No. of expatriates	(%)
Gender						
Male	11	(84.6)	158	(95.8)	169	(94.9)
Female	2	(15.4)	7	(4.2)	9	(5.1)
Age						
30-34	0		4	(2.4)	4	(2.2)
35-39	5	(38.5)	15	(9.1)	20	(11.2)
40-44	1	(7.7)	31	(18.8)	32	(18.0)
45-49	1	(7.7)	38	(23.0)	39	(21.9)
50-54	2	(15.4)	33	(20.0)	35	(19.7)
55-59	3	(23.1)	26	(15.8)	29	(16.3)
60 and above	1	(7.7)	18	(10.9)	19	(10.7)
Nationality						
American	4	(30.8)	21	(12.7)	25	(14.0)
Armenian	0		1	(0.6)	1	(0.6)
Australian	0		21	(12.7)	21	(11.8)
Austria	0		1	(0.6)	1	(0.6)
Belgian	0		3	(1.8)	3	(1.7)
British	5	(38.5)	47	(28.5)	52	(29.2)
Canadian	0		1	(0.6)	1	(0.6)
Danish	0		2	(1.2)	2	(1.1)
Dutch	0		13	(7.9)	13	(7.3)
French	0		15	(9.1)	15	(8.4)
French and Canadian	0		1	(0.6)	1	(0.6)
German	0		13	(7.9)	13	(7.3)
Greek	0		1	(0.6)	1	(0.6)
Indian	0		5	(3.0)	5	(2.8)
Irish	0		2	(1.2)	2	(1.1)
Israeli	0		1	(0.6)	1	(0.6)
Italian	0		1	(0.6)	1	(0.6)
Japanese	4	(30.8)	0		4	(2.2)
Malaysian	0		2	(1.2)	2	(1.1)
New Zealander	0		4	(2.4)	4	(2.2)
Norwegian	0		2	(1.2)	2	(1.1)
Pakistani	0		1	(0.6)	1	(0.6)
Sri Lankan	0		1	(0.6)	1	(0.6)
Swiss	0		5	(3.0)	5	(2.8)
Swiss and Danish	0		1	(0.6)	1	(0.6)
Industry sector						
Advertising, media and publishing	2	(15.4)	9	(5.5)	11	(6.2)
Aerospace	0		1	(0.6)	1	(0.6)
Architecture and interior design	0		3	(1.8)	3	(1.7)
Automotive	3	(23.1)	3	(1.8)	6	(3.3)
Banking and Financial services	2	(15.4)	10	(6.1)	12	(6.7)
Chemicals and Pharmaceuticals	0		2	(1.2)	2	(1.1)
Construction and real estate	4	(30.8)	7	(4.2)	11	(6.2)
Consumer goods	0		1	(0.6)	1	(0.6)
Consultancy (property, management, finance, accounting, tax, oil and gas)	1	(7.7)	14	(8.5)	15	(8.4)
Creative and art	0		2	(1.2)	2	(1.1)
Education	0		2	(1.2)	2	(1.1)
Food and agriculture	0		1	(0.6)	1	(0.6)
Healthcare	0		3	(1.8)	3	(1.7)

Hospitality and tourism	0		38	(23.0)	38	(21.3)
Insurance	0		3	(1.8)	3	(1.7)
IT	0		17	(10.3)	17	(9.5)
Legal Services	0		2	(1.2)	2	(1.1)
Business Services (accounting, audit, tax, legal advisory, recruitment)	0		11	(6.7)	11	(6.2)
Manufacturing	0		8	(4.8)	8	(4.5)
Marketing, market research and marketing recruitment	0		5	(3.0)	5	(2.8)
Oil and Gas	1	(7.7)	3	(1.8)	4	(2.2)
Pharmaceuticals and chemicals	0		2	(1.2)	2	(1.1)
Plastic packaging	0		1	(0.6)	1	(0.6)
Public (Government)	0		1	(0.6)	1	(0.6)
Research	0		2	(1.2)	2	(2.2)
Retail	0		2	(1.2)	2	(2.2)
Trading	0		1	(0.6)	1	(0.6)
Transportation and logistics	0		3	(1.8)	3	(1.7)
Work in more than one industry*	0		8	(4.8)	8	(4.5)
Job title						
CEO	13	(100)	20	(12.1)	33	(18.5)
Chief or Principle consultant	0		3	(1.8)	3	(1.7)
Director, Chief Officer or Head of a business function (e.g. finance, IT, design, operations, engineering, capital management)	0		38	(23.0)	38	(21.3)
Executive Chairman	0		5	(3.0)	5	(2.8)
General Manager	0		12	(7.3)	12	(6.7)
Regional President (Asia Pacific, South East Asia, Thailand)	0		8	(4.9)	8	(4.5)
Managing Director	0		48	(29.1)	48	(26.9)
Managing Partner	0		8	(4.9)	8	(4.5)
Vice president (sales and marketing, operations, revenue and strategy)	0		19	(11.5)	19	(10.6)
Others (e.g. Senior Manager)	0		4	(2.4)	4	(2.2)
No. of years worked in Thailand						
Less than 1	1	(7.7)	3	(1.8)	4	(2.2)
Between 1 and 2	1	(7.7)	16	(9.7)	17	(9.6)
Between 2.1 and 5		(0)	37	(22.4)	37	(20.8)
Between 5.1 and 10	3	(23.1)	44	(26.7)	47	(26.4)
Between 10.1 and 15	2	(15.4)	28	(17.0)	30	(16.9)
More than 15	6	(46.2)	37	(22.4)	43	(24.1)

Note:
*: Some expatriates work in more than one industry. For example, one expatriate works in Automotive, Oil and Gas, and Construction; another in Automotive, Power Equipment, and Food.

Chapter Three Executive Summary
The Study Methodology

- This book is based on data and information collected through semi-structured interviews and a qualitative on-line survey from 178 expatriate senior business leaders working in Thailand.

- The expatriates held senior positions in their organizations, including job titles such as CEO, CFO, director, chairman, managing director, president, senior vice president and general manager. They spanned 25 different nationalities and work in over 30 industries.

- The majority of the expatriates were male (94.9%), over three-quarters (75.9%) were between 40 and 59 years old, and about two-thirds (67.4%) had worked in Thailand for more than five years. 24.1% had worked there for more than 15 years.

PART II.
THAILAND: AN OVERVIEW

CHAPTER 4. THAILAND'S HISTORICAL, POLITICAL AND ECONOMIC BACKGROUND

The key task of a business leader is to achieve business goals through effective people management. To effectively manage/lead Thai employees, it is essential to have a good understanding of their values, norms, attitudes, and behaviours, all of which are shaped by the historical, political, economic, and social environment to which they belong. This chapter provides an overview of Thailand's historical, political, and economic background; the next one focusses on the key Thai cultural values to help understand the work attitudes and behaviours of Thai employees.

THAILAND'S HISTORICAL AND POLITICAL BACKGROUND

Until 1939, the kingdom of Thailand was known as Siam. Thailand is the only country in Southeast Asia never to have been under colonial rule, which helped preserve its unique culture. The country's historical past, its monarchy, its military, and the Buddhist religion have shaped its society and politics, which, in turn, influence the work values, attitudes and behaviours of Thai employees.

Thailand is a constitutional monarchy in which the King functions as the head of state and the Prime Minister serves as the head of government. This form of government was established in 1932, following nearly 700 years of rule by various dynasties of Thai monarchs. The current King, Maha Vajiralongkorn, succeeded to the throne of Thailand after his father's death on 13 October 2016. The former King, Bhumibol Adulyadej was, at the time of his death, the longest reigning King in Thailand's history, serving 70 years, and the world's longest-reigning monarch.

In Thailand, respect for the Royal Family goes beyond mere social custom; under lèse majesté laws, negative or defamatory comments about or threats towards the members of the Royal Family can lead to arrest and to being deported or sentenced to three to 15 years imprisonment. Section 112 of Thailand's criminal code states that

"Whoever, defames, insults, or threatens the King, the Queen, the Heir-apparent, or the Regent shall be punished with imprisonment of three to fifteen years". The images of the King are expected to be treated with almost as much respect as the King himself.

Thailand has experienced several coup d'états since becoming a constitutional monarchy. The country's military has overthrown the government and seized power 12 times; most recently in 2014, when then Prime Minster Yinglak Chinnawa was removed and the head of the Royal Thai Army, General Prayuth Chan-ocha (the current prime minister) seized power.

POPULATION, RELIGION AND LANGUAGE

Population Thailand's population is approximately 65.73 million (2015 est.), and is mainly composed of Thais (95.9%), the remainder being made up of Burmese (2%) and other nationalities (2.1%). The ethnic composition includes Chinese, Malays, Cambodians, Vietnamese, Indians, and others. The size of Thailand's work force is of 38.70 million (June 2016), roughly one-third (35.1%) of which is occupied in the agricultural sector (BoI, 2016a; NSO, 2016a).

Religion Buddhism is Thailand's predominant religion, being followed by over 93.6% of the population. The rest of the population is affiliated to Islam (4.9%), Christianity (1.2%), and other religions (0.2%). Although the vast majority of the people of Thailand are Buddhist, the country practices freedom of religion, with all faiths being protected by the Thai constitution. Buddhist values are a part of Thai daily life; temples, monasteries and images of the Buddha can be seen everywhere. Buddhist values and teachings wield a strong influence on Thai attitudes and behaviours in relation to both work and life. For example, the Middle Way value guides Thais to seek balance in their life, work, family, and everyday actions (Chompookum & Brooklyn Derr, 2004). Thais consider the image of the Buddha to be sacred and treat it with extreme respect.

Language and Literacy Although Thai is the official language of Thailand, English is widely used in larger companies; however, proficiency in the latter is low among small and medium-sized enterprises (SMEs) and the lower-tiers of the workforce. The literacy rate in Thailand is quite high, with 98.2% of the population being able to read and write (NSO, 2016b).

THAILAND'S ECONOMY

With a GDP of USD395.2 billion (2015) and per capita GDP of USD5,878.2 (2015), the Thai economy is ranked as the 31st largest in the world (BoI, 2016c) and the 2nd largest in Southeast Asia, after Indonesia. The country's GDP yearly growth averaged 2.1% between 2013 and 2015. Thailand's GDP derives from agriculture (10.4%), industry (37.7%), and services (51.9%) (2015 est.) (CIA, 2016).

Exports are the main contributors to Thailand's economy, accounting for 60% of its GDP and enabling the country to be ranked as the 24th largest exporter in the world in 2016. Agricultural and manufacturing products are the two main export outputs, being ranked as the world's 11th and 16th largest respectively (BoI, 2016c). Examples of the products exported and their world rankings (2014 data) are shown below:

- Rice **#1**
- Pineapple **#2**
- Sugar **#2**
- Cassava **#1**
- Rubber **#1**
- Rubber tires**#6**
- Computing devices **#7**
- Computer accessories **#9**
- Motorcycles **#7**
- Trucks **#5**
- HDDs **#1**

Source: The Board of Investment of Thailand (BOI, 2016c)

Foreign Direct Investment (FDI) Policies Having transformed itself from a primarily agriculture-based economy to an export-led one, several factors have contributed to Thailand's current status: a well-developed infrastructure, a market-driven economy, inexpensive labour, and pro-investment policies.

In terms of Foreign Direct Investment (FDI) policies, the Thai government plays a promoting and supporting role and actively welcomes those foreign investments that contribute to the development of skills, technology, innovation, and economy (e.g., through tax incentives, support services, and import duty exemptions or reductions). The Board of Investment states that "In fact, government approval to invest in Thailand is not even needed unless the special incentives offered by the Board of Investment are being applied for, and most sectors of the Thai economy are open to foreign investors".

Thailand was ranked 49th out of 189 nations by the World Bank's 2016 Ease of Doing Business survey (WorldBank, 2016a) and 8th best FDI host country in the world for 2014-2016 by the United Nations Conference on Trade and development (UNCTAD, 2016).

Future economic growth projections Against the backdrop of the slow 2013-15 economic growth resulting from the May 2014 coup d'état and sluggish foreign demand, particularly from China and other Asian economies, the Fiscal Policy Office has reported that the Thai GDP is projected to grow by 3.3% in 2016 (BoI, 2016b). This growth is expected to be driven by the USD9.52 billion economic stimulus measures announced in September 2015 (FocusEconomics, 2015).

Unemployment Rate Thailand's unemployment rate is among the lowest in the world, with an average of 1.04% over the 2005-2015 period (WorldBank, 2016b). A study conducted by the International Labour Organization (ILO) on workforce shortages and admission of foreign workers to Thailand shows that the country is facing workforce shortages and has absorbed huge numbers (estimated at more than two million) of migrant workers from neighbouring countries to work in the agriculture, manufacturing, and services sectors (Ducanes & Abella, 2013). It is projected that, from 2020 to 2030, Thailand's working-age population will decline at a yearly rate of 150,000 workers, which may lead to even more serious workforce shortages and an ever higher dependence on foreign workers (Ducanes & Abella, 2013).

STATISTICS ON BUSINESS ESTABLISHMENT IN THAILAND

The recent industrial census conducted by Thailand's National Statistical Office in 2012 shows that there were 2.3 million business establishments in Thailand. This section presents the statistics pertaining to the number, size, legal status, foreign ownership of and people engaged and employed in business establishments.

Number of Establishments by Sector Over one-third (35.7%) of all business establishments were engaged in retail and nearly one-fifth (18.7%) in manufacturing. Figure 1 shows the percentage of establishments operating in different economic activities.

Figure 1. Percentage of establishments by economic activities

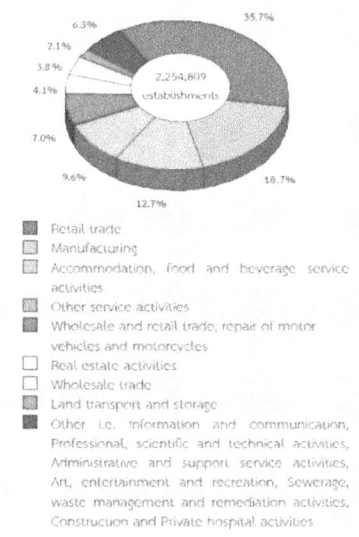

Source: Industrial Census 2012, National Statistical Office (NSO, 2016)

Size of Establishments The overall size of establishments, measured by the number of people employed, was small, with 97.3% of them employing no more than 15 people.

Figure 2. Number of establishments by size

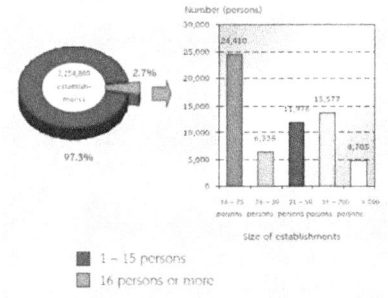

Source: Industrial Census 2012, National Statistical Office (NSO, 2016)

Form of Legal Organization The majority of the establishments (about 92.4%) were owned by individual proprietors. Limited and public limited companies only accounted for 4.9%.

Figure 3. Percentage of establishment by form of legal organization

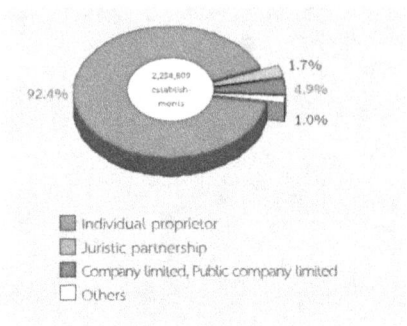

Source: Industrial Census 2012, National Statistical Office (NSO, 2016)

Foreign Investment or Share Holding The limited and public limited companies were predominantly (96.8%) owned by Thai nationals; only 3.2% had foreign- or shared-ownership. Over half of the foreign- or shared-ownership establishments (56.7%) were 10-50% shared and a quarter (25.8%) were more than 50% shared.

Figure 4. Percentage of corporate establishments by proportion of foreign investment or share holding

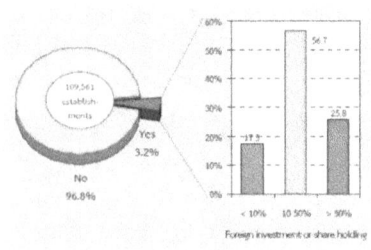

Source: Industrial Census 2012, National Statistical Office (NSO, 2016)

Number of Persons Engaged and Employed by Economic Activity
Looking at the numbers of people *engaged* (including owners or business partners, unpaid workers and employees in the establishments) and people *employed* in different sectors shown in Figure 5, we can see that a high proportion of the workforce was found in the manufacturing sector. About 4.4 million people or 42.5% were engaged in manufacturing (3.7 million people or 52.8% employed). Following these, 1.9 million persons or 18.2% were engaged in retail (671 thousand people or 9.6% employed), and 1.0 million people or 9.8% were engaged in accommodation, and food and beverage service activities (577 thousand people or 8.3% employed).

Figure 5 Number of person engaged and employed by economic activity

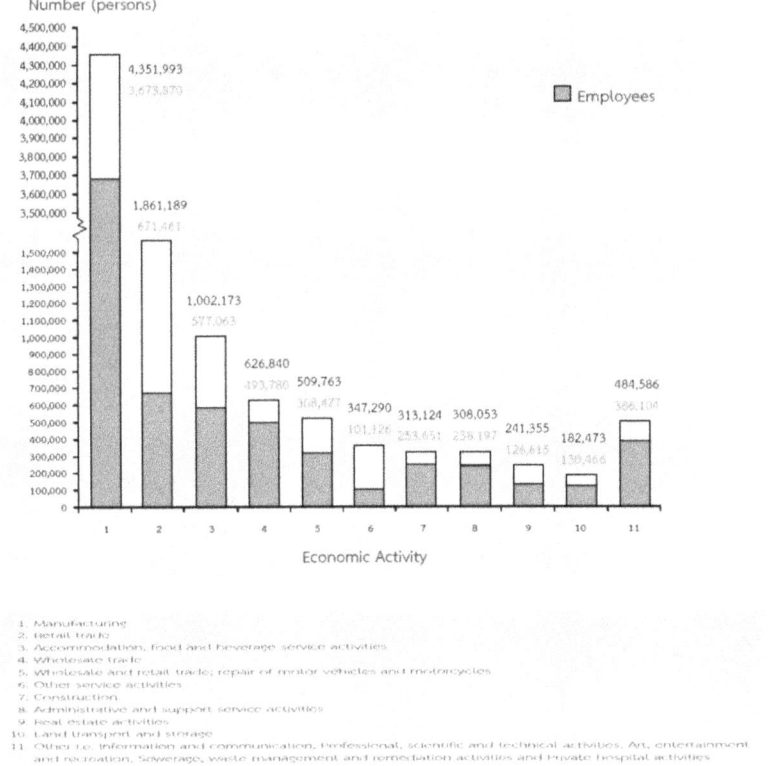

1. Manufacturing
2. Retail trade
3. Accommodation, food and beverage service activities
4. Wholesale trade
5. Wholesale and retail trade; repair of motor vehicles and motorcycles
6. Other service activities
7. Construction
8. Administrative and support service activities
9. Real estate activities
10. Land transport and storage
11. Other i.e. information and communication, professional, scientific and technical activities, Art, entertainment and recreation, Sewerage, waste management and remediation activities and Private hospital activities

Source: Industrial Census 2012, National Statistical Office (NSO, 2016)

The census data presented above show that Thailand's business establishments are predominately small in size (employing no more than 15 people) and owned by Thai nationals. Over half of the workforce (52.8%) is employed in manufacturing, followed by 9.6% in retail and 8.3% in accommodation, food and beverage service activities.

Chapter Four Executive Summary
Thailand's Historical, Political and Economic Background

- To effectively manage/lead Thai employees, it is essential to have a good understanding of their values, norms, attitudes and behaviours. All of these are influenced by their historical, political, economic, and social environment.

- Thailand's historical past, its monarchy, its military, and the Buddhist religion have shaped its society and politics, which, in turn, influence the work values, attitudes and behaviours of Thai employees.

- Thailand is a constitutional monarchy, in which the King functions as the head of state and the Prime Minister serves as the head of government.

- Buddhism is Thailand's predominant religion, being followed by over 93.6% of the population. Buddhist values and teachings have a strong influence on the Thais' attitudes and behaviours with regard to both work and life.

- The Thai economy is ranked as the 31st largest in the world, with a GDP of USD395.2 billion (2015) and a per capita GDP of $5,878.2 (2015). Exports are the main contributors to Thailand's economy, accounting for 60% of its GDP; agricultural and manufacturing products are the country's two main export outputs.

- Thailand's unemployment rate is among the lowest in the world, with an average of 1.04% over the 2005-2015 period. Thailand faces labour shortages and has absorbed a huge number (estimated at more than 2 million) of migrant workers from neighbouring countries to work in the agriculture, manufacturing, and services sectors.

- The recent industrial census of 2012, conducted by the National Statistical Office, shows that Thailand was home to 2.3 million business establishments. Those business establishments were predominately small in size (employing no more than 15 people) and owned by Thai nationals. Over half of the workforce (52.8%) was employed in manufacturing, followed by 9.6% in retail and 8.3% in the accommodation, food, and beverage services.

CHAPTER 5. KEY THAI CULTURAL VALUES

To understand the work attitudes and behaviours of Thai employees, one must explore their values. This chapter presents the key cultural values held by Thai people as described in the literature. An empirical account of the values and characteristics of Thai employees from the perspectives of the 178 expatriates is presented in chapter 6.

DEEP RESPECT FOR AGE, RANK AND SENIORITY

The Thai social structure can be seen as a vertical hierarchy in which members of society are ranked according to their status, seniority, and authority. A person's place within this hierarchy is determined by both ascribed (age, birth, family background) and achieved criteria (education, position in work, wealth, power) (Pornpitakpan, 2000). From a young age, Thais are taught that parents are superior to children and that bosses are superior to subordinates. They are also taught to honour their parents and respect their elders and superiors. Under this hierarchical structure, the Thai people take rank, age, and seniority seriously and give respect to those holding higher social status and to the elderly. Those holding lower rank are expected to show restraint and comply with the requests of those who they perceive as being superior to avoid offending them.

In line with this hierarchical structure, senior managers often assume an authoritarian stance in the workplace context, making decisions and issuing orders with little consultation of their subordinates (Pornpitakpan, 2000). This management tradition, however, has made most Thai employees accustomed to relying on instructions from the top and to rarely taking initiatives (ExpatArrivals, 2016). Promotions are often based on candidate seniority rather than performance; thus, top-level jobs are often held by older individuals.

THE HIGH VALUE PLACED ON 'FACE'

The concept of 'face' may not be unfamiliar to expatriates who have worked in Asian countries, but could be alien to those coming to Asia for the first time. In Asian societies, 'face' is seen as a key variable that has a pervasive and significant influence on social interactions and human behaviours, from individual decision making to national policy setting (Kim & Nam, 1998). It is thus important for managers from the West to have knowledge of this concept in order to understand much of their Asian employees' behaviour.

The concept of 'face' originated in China and is an abstract and intangible concept that has no universal definition. It has been conceptualised in many ways; for example, it is variously seen as "a reputation achieved through getting on in life, through success and ostentation" (Hu, 1944:45), "a social esteem accorded by others" (Yang, 1945:167), "an image of self-delineated in terms of approved social attributes" (Goffman, 1955:213), and "the respectability and/or deference which a person can claim for himself from others, by virtue of the relative position he occupies in his social network and the degree to which he is judged to have functioned adequately in that position as well as acceptably in his general conduct" (Ho, 1976:883). From the above, we can see that the concept of 'face' can represent one's own sense of reputation, esteem, pride, prestige, image, and respectability in a social context.

'Face' is highly valued by Thais, it is carefully protected and maintained; most people will go to any length to avoid losing face. For example, some Thai employees may withhold information or cover mistakes in order to keep intact their reputation or those of others. There are a number of situations that may cause a Thai employee to feel that he or she is losing face; for example, being publicly rejected, questioned, or criticised; being exposed as lacking in knowledge or ability; failing to fulfil one's social duties; and being the object of a dismissive gesture from a supervisor or of mockery from a colleague. The concept of 'saving face' is regarded as one of the major issues linked to leading/managing Thai employees; thus, several sections in this book will illustrate how issues related to 'face' influence the ways in which expatriate managers lead/manage Thai employees.

HIGH COLLECTIVISM, EXTERNAL LOCUS OF CONTROL, AND BELIEF IN PREDESTINED FATE

Thais tend to be collectivistic, to hold high degrees of collective responsibility for their family members, and to emphasize interdependence, conformity, belongingness, and obedience (Pornpitakpan, 2000). Because of these collective traits, individual decisions and actions are often influenced by family members and peers. Many Thais perceive that it is important to gain the approval of the members of their immediate community before making decisions and taking actions (C. Lee & Green, 1991; Pornpitakpan, 2000; Thorelli & Sentell, 1982). As a result of this collective orientation, they believe that their future is not under their control, which shows the characteristics of an *external* locus of control.

Locus of control refers to the degree to which individuals perceive they can control their decisions and lives. Locus of control theory (Rotter, 1966, 1975) identifies two types of people. The first type, who have a strong *external* locus of control, believe in *external* control, i.e., that what happens to them is beyond their control and is the result of luck, fate, chance, or the power of others; thus, they tend to attribute outcomes of events to external circumstances. The second, who have an *internal* locus of control, believe that the events in their lives are contingent on their own behaviours, abilities, efforts or attributes; thus, they tend to attribute the outcomes of events to their own actions.

Several studies found that, compared to their western counterparts, Thais tend to believe in a more external locus of control and are thus more fatalistic; believing that events and outcomes are determined in advance and cannot be changed (Komin, 1990; Pornpitakpan, 2000; Thorelli & Sentell, 1982). It was found that beliefs in spirits, predestined fate, and supernatural power are prevalent in Thailand. Buddhism, the predominant religion of Thailand, is one of the key forces influencing the Thais' belief in fatalism. For example, Buddhism teaches that the world and the human body and thought are a compound that is subject to the influence of nature and surrounding conditions. Human existence is seen as suffering and a person's current situation is seen as linked to the actions committed in previous lives. Thus, people should not complain about their predetermined fate, but should perform good deeds in their current lives so that their next ones will be better.

The Thai employees' characteristics of fatalism and belief in an external locus of control have two significant implications for the management of their performance. First, Thai employees may be less ambitious than their western counterparts in seeking achievement in their working life. Research has showed that people with different beliefs in locus of control have different levels of need for achievement; external locus being linked with lower levels of need for achievement. Given that Thais tend to believe that what happens to them is not under their control—specifically with regard to their position in the workplace—they may not be keen to progress up the organisational hierarchy. Second, employee motivation theory—such as Victor Vroom's expectancy theory—indicates that the prospect of attractive rewards will motivate employees to put in sufficient efforts in order to achieve performance targets. However, in Thai workplaces, the use of rewards to try to enhance Thai employees' motivations, efforts, and performances may not be effective because many Thais believe that their performance is not only influenced by their efforts but also by chance and luck (Pornpitakpan, 2000).

THE PERCEPTION THAT BUILDING GOOD INTERPERSONAL RELATIONSHIPS IS ESSENTIAL

Thai culture places a high importance on maintaining good and harmonious interpersonal relationships (Chompookum & Brooklyn Derr, 2004; Pornpitakpan, 2000) which are seen as one of the cornerstones of Thai society (Holmes, Tangtongtavy, & Tomizawa, 1995). Various guides to doing business in Thailand emphasise the importance of building good interpersonal relationships with Thai business contacts and counterparts, as Thai people prefer to do business with people they know, trust, and respect (see, e.g., Austrade, 2016; Nlambassade, 2016; UKTI, 2016). The same is true for leading and managing Thai employees. Thai employees like to work with/for people they trust and respect. Maintaining good interpersonal relationships with Thai subordinates and obtaining their trust and respect can greatly help establish more cooperative working relationships.

Thais often categorise people into in-group and out-group members; the former usually include their family members, colleagues and those others with whom they usually come into contact, while the latter include everyone else. Thais are generally nice to their in-group members, but may behave uncooperatively towards out-group members (Pornpitakpan, 2000). It is thus suggested that expatriates working with Thais should try to build good relationships with their Thai colleagues (Pornpitakpan, 2000). Examples of ways to establish such good relationships include dining together, participating in social events, and sending personalised gifts or cards.

HIGHLY CONTEXTUAL AND INDIRECT COMMUNICATION

When comparing the styles of communication adopted in Thailand with those in western countries, two aspects are often considered: 1) high- or low-context based communication and 2) direct vs. indirect communication.

High- or Low-Context Based Communication When communication is low-context based, the conveyed information and message are clearly expressed in the words; conversely, when it is high-context based, the conveyance of the message's meaning, beyond the words used, depends heavily on contextual and social cues (Pornpitakpan, 2000; Simintiras & Thomas, 1998; Thatcher, 2001). Thai communication is found to be highly contextual, with most of the message's meaning being conveyed through non-verbal cues, such as facial expressions, similes, gestures, pauses, and body movements, while very little is in what is actually spoken. Expatriates accustomed to the 'spelling out your thoughts' communication approach would find that the Thais' highly contextual communication style often makes the communicated message confusing or difficult to understand.

In order for expatriates working with Thais to understand what is really being said, it has been suggested that they need to learn to understand and read non-verbal cues, pay attention to *how* things are said, and bear in mind the concept that explicit words are often inadequate (Pornpitakpan, 2000). Expatriates also need to be mindful of their own facial expressions and body language, as most Thais will look for unspoken cues and see them as more important than what is being said.

Direct vs. Indirect Communication The Thai way of communicating tends to be indirect and reserved, which is in contrast with the direct and self-assertive style valued in many western countries. Several Thai cultural communicative norms, such as conflict avoidance, emotional control, display of respect, modesty, and politeness (Sriussadaporn, 2006), have fostered the development of such indirectness in communication. The norms are mainly aimed at maintaining and/or enhancing interpersonal harmony (Pornpitakpan, 2000). However, they have made most Thai employees inclined to avoid confrontation and direct criticism (even of the constructive variety) and to adopt a non-assertive, humble, and indirect approach (Pornpitakpan, 2000).

Their cultural norms and values also make Thai employees inclined to rarely challenge the viewpoints and instructions of their supervisors or to refuse the latter's requests even when they are unsure of being able to carry them out (Sriussadaporn, 2006). Thus, the word 'yes' ('Chai' in Thai, with the polite forms 'Khrap' for men or 'Kha' for women) is often heard. But 'yes' does not always imply agreement. In many cases, it is best translated as "yes, I follow you" (Nlambassade, 2016). To avoid misunderstanding, it is suggested best to check whether the response is actually "yes, I agree".

Given the Thais' trait of indirectness in communication, some Thais may perceive the expatriates' direct communication style as offensive; on the other hand, some expatriates working with Thais may become irritated or confused by the latter's indirectness. It has been suggested that, when communicating with Thais, a soft and polite approach will work better than a direct and straightforward one (Pornpitakpan, 2000). In addition, reading between the lines is necessary to understand what is really being said.

Chapter Five Executive Summary
Key Thai Cultural Values

- To help understand the work attitudes and behaviours of Thai employees, this chapter presents a review of the literature on the cultural values and characteristics of the Thai people.

- Based on my review of the literature, Thai employees have the following key characteristics:

Deep Respect for Age, Rank and Seniority: Thai people take age, rank, and seniority seriously and respect the elderly and those of higher social status. Those of lower standing are expected to show restraint and oblige the requests of those they perceive as superiors to avoid offending them. In line with this hierarchical structure, senior managers often assume an authoritarian role in the workplace context, making decisions and issuing orders with little consultation of their subordinates.This management tradition, however, has led most Thai employees to become accustomed to relying on instructions from the top and to rarely take initiatives

High Value Placed on 'Face': The concept of 'face' can be seen as a person's own sense of reputation, esteem, pride, prestige, image, and respectability in a social context. 'Face' is highly valued by Thais; it is carefully protected and maintained. Most people will go to any length to avoid losing face.

High Collectivism, External Locus of Control and Belief in Predestined Fate: Thais tend to be collectivistic and emphasize interdependence, conformity, belongingness, and obedience. When compared with their western counterparts, several studies found that Thais tend to believe in *external* locus of control and are more fatalistic, believing that what happens to them is beyond their control and is the result of luck, fate, chance, or the power of others. These characteristics may have led Thai employees to become less ambitious in seeking achievement in their working life and may make the use of rewards to try to enhance their motivation, effort, and performance less effective.

The Perception that Building Good Interpersonal Relationships is Essential:
Thai culture places a high importance on maintaining good and harmonious interpersonal relationships. Thai employees

like to work with/for people they trust and respect. Maintaining good interpersonal relationships with Thai subordinates and obtaining their trust and respect can greatly help establish more cooperative working relationships.

Highly contextual and Indirect Communication: Thai communication is found to be highly contextual; most of the message is conveyed through non-verbal cues, such as facial expressions, similes, gestures, pauses, and body movements, while very little is in the words that are actually spoken. In order for expatriates working with Thais to understand what is actually being said, it has been suggested that they need to learn to understand and read non-verbal cues, pay attention to *how* things are said, and bear in mind the concept that explicit words are often inadequate.

The Thai way of communicating tends to be indirect and reserved. Several cultural Thai communicative norms, such as conflict avoidance, emotional control, display of respect, modesty, and politeness (Sriussadaporn, 2006) have fostered the development of this indirectness in communication. The norms are mainly aimed at maintaining and/or enhancing interpersonal harmony. However, they have made most Thai employees inclined to avoid confrontation and direct criticism (even of the constructive variety) and to adopt a non-assertive, humble and indirect approach (Pornpitakpan, 2000).

PART III.
VIEWS AND EXPERIENCES OF THE 178 EXPATRIATE SENIOR MANAGERS

CHAPTER 6.
CHARACTERISTICS OF THAI EMPLOYEES

Over 90% of the expatriate managers said that leading Thai subordinates was very different from leading their counterparts in their home countries, and that a number of unique characteristics of Thai employees had a great influence on the way they led/managed them. Here I report the five characteristics most mentioned by the expatriates to show how they had influenced their leadership approaches.

INEXPRESSIVENESS

One of the most mentioned characteristic of Thai employees was their inexpressiveness, their unwillingness to speak their minds, and their tendency to keep things to themselves. This had presented a challenge for the expatriates as they were unable to understand the viewpoints of their subordinates and the reasoning behind the Thai managers' decisions. This inexpressiveness was thought to be the result of a combination of hierarchy, religious beliefs and face-saving.

Hierarchy is prevalent in Thai society and workplaces (Jingjit & Fotaki, 2011; Siengthi & Bechter, 2004). Many expatriates expressed that they had found it difficult to get their subordinates to speak their minds due to the prevalent hierarchical management tradition. They stated that Thais respected authority and seniority to the extent that subordinates or juniors did not question authority in the decision-making process and would provide the answers that their managers expected to hear. A French expatriate stated:

> The Thai are more likely to consider work as an extension of family. This means [that their] superior is [a] mentor/father/mother figure [...] Thai society, being strongly based on hierarchy, [sees] the superior [as being] "always right". The young do not criticized old. The boss is "supposed to know" and the Thai will "Kreng Jai" [it means showing respect,

politeness and consideration towards others], show their respect
for harmony by providing the expected answers, not necessarily
their real opinions.
(French expatriate, 35-39 years old, Manufacturing)

Inexpressiveness is considered to be both an outcome and a reinforcement of the hierarchical system, as hierarchy makes employees inexpressive towards their managers, which reinforces the hierarchical system. One Japanese expatriate said:

The gap between senior management and employees is too wide
[...] They [the workers] feel they are too small and too inferior to
associate themselves with the senior managers; so they [the
workers] tend not to speak up. By not speaking up, they tend to
widen the gap further.
(Japanese expatriate, 35-39 years old, Auto manufacturing)

Hierarchy was seen by the expatriates as an obstacle to organizational effectiveness and, in some cases, making project work impossible, as senior Thais would not work on projects with anyone younger and less experienced. More findings related to hierarchy and seniority are discussed in the next section.

In addition to hierarchy, many respondents believed that Buddhism had a profound influence on the way Thais work and their interaction with management, as over 90% of the population is Buddhist. *Karma*, a dogma in Buddhism, was mentioned by the respondents as having a significant influence on behavior. The 'doctrine of karma [is] an explanation for how certain aspects of one's present experience are consequences of previous acts, including acts in former existences, and an incentive to perform certain acts which will ensure greater freedom from suffering in this life or future ones' (Keyes, 1989: 122). Thais therefore generally accept their fate and did not question leaders.

Another reason for the Thais' unwillingness to speak up is to save their own and others' 'face'. A British expatriate said that the employees were unwilling to inform the management about any problems in order to save face, as they thought that, had they said there was something wrong, it would have reflected badly on them. An American expatriate stated his view on why the Thais were inexpressive:

One, they don't want to embarrass themselves. Two, they don't
want to show off because they might make somebody else look
bad.
(American expatriate, 55-59 years old, Banking sector)

34

RESPECT FOR SENIORITY AND HIERARCHY

One of the first things many expatriate senior managers observed when they first arrived in Thailand was that Thai employees are very respectful towards older people and people higher up in the organisational hierarchy. In Thailand, there is strong age-based hierarchy. In some Western countries, older people may be side-lined whereas, in Thailand, age and greying hair represent experience and knowledge and are deemed to be worthy of respect. Two expatriates stated:

> *[...] age and grey hair generally provide the inference of having experience and 'venerable' knowledge.*
> (Australian expatriate, 60 or over years old, Logistics & Transport Services)

> *In Thailand, I am respected for my knowledge; they truly want to learn from me. Age is not a question, or an issue, the Thais have more respect for age.*
> (New Zealander expatriate, 55–59 years old, Marketing and Diplomatic Agent)

The Thai employees' respect for seniority, however, have posed several challenges when leading them. Below, I present the key challenges, as perceived by the expatriates.

Challenge a. Seniority is Seen as More Important than Competency and Performance. Some of the expatriates observed that Thai people respect seniority regardless of ability. Such emphasis on seniority has long been applied to performance appraisal in the Thai workplace. As a common practice, pay and benefits often rise with age and length of service, whereas an individual's competency and performance are less taken into account.

Some expatriates stated that Thai employees 'expect' promotions and pay rises just for doing the same job longer than their peers, rather than for showing more competency in their work. This becomes a significant challenge for organisational performance as it results in people moving to more senior positions without demonstrable performance track records. An expatriate stated that this phenomenon can be observed by simply reviewing the CVs of Thai job applicants. He said,

> *[...] you will notice the following symptoms: a) candidates often emphasise 'responsibilities' rather than 'achievements'; and b) candidates applying for more senior positions often present*

responsibilities that are not much different from [those of] candidates applying for more junior positions.
(Malaysia expatriate, 40-44 years old, Oil and Gas sector)

Some of the expatriates worried that such emphasis on seniority, rather than competency and performance, could seriously undermine the sustainability of a business.

Challenge b. Difficulty for a Younger Thai Employee to Manage or Supervise an Older Colleague.   Another challenge arising from the Thai employees' respect for seniority and hierarchy involved capable and knowledgeable younger workers struggling to lead people older than themselves. As mentioned earlier, hierarchy may make project work impossible as senior Thais will not work on projects under anyone younger and less experienced. Thus, the seniority and hierarchy system makes it difficult for younger employees with abilities and competencies similar or better than those of older employees to progress in their careers. An American expatriate stated,

> *In Thailand, age and year of graduation are very important when deciding who gets promoted. It is very difficult for a younger Thai to manage or supervise an older Thai.*
> (American Expatriate, 60 or over years old, High-Tech)

Challenge c. Respect for Seniority and Authority Has Become a Constraint to Open Communication and Sharing of Ideas. The Thai employees' respect and obedience towards authority and higher ranking people lead them to hardly ever express their views and challenge their superiors. This is seen by the expatriates as an inhibiting factor to sharing ideas and creating an open communication work environment. The following statements illustrate this challenge:

> *Thai society has its hierarchy, in which a junior never questions a senior. This is ingrained in the social structure and it is sometimes very counterproductive to creating open ideas.*
> (Indian Expatriate, 30–34 years old, IT)

> *Getting Thai colleagues to contribute an opinion, particularly when it is in opposition to one expressed by senior colleagues, is nearly impossible.*
> (Pakistani Expatriate, 50–54 years old, Research)

Thai structures work by seniority and you have to obey the older person. People do not speak up like they do in the Western world. So it is more difficult to create a work environment of open communication.

(Australian Expatriate, 40–44 years old, Hospitality)

Challenge d. Thai Employees Tend to Follow Orders but not to Challenge Instructions. Another challenge resulting from the Thai employees' respect for seniority and authority is that they tend to scrupulously follow their superiors' instructions but seldom question the reasons for doing a job or challenge the instructions or directions given to them.

[…] a Thai would not openly challenge a 'senior' or one in power. And will follow word for word what is dictated by Senior Management

(British Expatriate, 60 or over years old, HR and Training, Oil & Gas Consultancy)

Generally, team members are less outspoken and "follow managers in an almost army-like fashion", meaning that hardly anybody ever objects, even though the provided leadership is sub-optimal.

(German Expatriate, 50–54 years old, IT)

The Thai employees' respect for seniority has both good and bad implications. A good one is that leaders do not need to take the time to explain the reasons for their instructions in order to convince their staff. A bad one is that instructions or orders, both good and bad, given by higher organisational ranks are not challenged by Thai employees as they will mostly just accept them. Thus, in most situations, the interaction between managers and subordinates become top-down, with managers giving instructions and subordinates following them.

The Thai employees' deep-rooted belief in compliance, obedience and in not challenging their supervisors (even when they know that their supervisors are wrong) could be alien to many expatriate managers who were born and raised in the West; it is therefore a management issue of which to be aware.

THE GREAT IMPORTANCE OF SAVING FACE

The concept of 'face' can be seen as one's own sense of reputation, esteem, pride, prestige, image and respectability in a social context, as explained in chapter 5.

Many expatriates said that their Thai employees see 'face' as something that is extremely important to uphold. Thai staff may resign should they lose face. As an Australian expatriate said, losing face in the East is akin to feeling shame in the West.

> *Never underestimate the value of 'face', losing face with friends, colleagues – anyone. It's immensely powerful, akin to maximum shame in the West.*
> (Australian Expatriate, 45–49 years old, Auto industry)

The following statement from a British expatriate, ironically illustrates the importance of 'face' to Thai employees,

> *[I] never have to sack anyone, I just make them lose face in front of their colleagues and their resignation is very swift.*
> (British Expatriate, 50–54 years old, Hospitality)

The Thai employees' preoccupation with avoiding losing face has led to some behaviours that are uncommon to and may not be accepted in Western workplaces. For example, Thai employees tend not to speak in meetings as they don't want to say something wrong, which would cause them to become embarrassed and make them lose face; saving one's own 'face' could take priority over team and company; in order save face, excuses or false evidence may be used to deny association with any mistakes they made.

An Australian expatriate expressed that the importance ascribed by Thai subordinates to saving face was one of the key issues in leading them. He said,

> *The saving face issue is a major issue when dealing with Thais [...] If you publicly confront employees when something goes wrong, they will deny any association, even with compelling evidence. The employees could resign if they lost face [...] Thais will also rarely reveal issues they are dealing with, as this may lead them to losing face.*
> (Australian expatriate, 50-54 years old, IT services)

The 'face' issue makes Thai employees behave differently from those in the West in the workplace; thus, the way in which to lead employees in Thailand is influenced by the issue of 'face'. An American expatriate said,

> *Leading Thai employees is very different because of the whole issue of 'face' and status.*
> (American expatriate, 40–44 years old, Market Research)

Many expatriates said that they had to adjust their management style to accommodate the issue of 'face'. An Australian expatriate expressed that the concept of 'saving face' can be a strong inhibitor to a successful business culture as the risk of losing face seems to hold back many Thai employees from taking initiatives. Many expatriates also said that understanding the concept of 'face' and being able to save the face of employees is one of the keys to success in Thailand. An Austrian expatriate expressed:

> *I personally have worked with Thai nationals a very long time and it has now become second nature. In my humble opinion, it is a matter of 'not losing face'. I am a strong believer that [foreign nationals] working with Thai nationals should take time and [make an] effort to learn about the culture and, in doing so, have the ability to gain a deeper understanding of Thai society.*
> (Austrian expatriate, 50–54 years old, Hospitality)

LIMITED INITIATIVE AND ANALYTICAL ABILITY

Another frequently mentioned characteristic was the Thai employees' lack of initiative and analytical ability. Many expatriates pointed out that most Thai employees expect to be given detailed instructions as to how to complete a task and that the ability to follow a logical train of thought to a logical conclusion is absent in most of them.

The following quotes illustrate some of the expatriates' views:

> *Tasks are prone to get stuck as no one takes any initiative [...] they often prefer to be dictated rather than think [for themselves].*
> (American expatriate, 30–34 years old, Telecommunications)

> *Problem solving and analytical abilities are very weak: they tend to cut and paste data and are unable to critique it. This is true even of employees who have Master's degrees.*
> (Austrian expatriate, 45–49 years old, Hospitality)

In my home country (Australia), employees generally use more initiative and are [more capable of solving] problems [...] without relying on senior management assistance. In Thailand, employees don't tend to be as proactive.

(Australian expatriate, 35–39 years old, Food Manufacturing and Export)

Thai employees show a lot less initiative and creative thinking. Socially, the boss is seen as superior and employees want to follow instructions rather than come up with solutions themselves.

(British expatriate, 50–54 years old, Recruitment)

Thus, one of the major challenges for the expatriate leaders was to encourage their Thai staff to take initiatives and dare to go ahead with a task without having to instruct them on how to do so.

This characteristic is thought to be the result of the rote learning approach used in Thai education institutions. Thai students often learn or memorise things by repetition, without an understanding of the reasoning or relationships involved in the material that is learned. Two expatriates stated the following:

Thailand's 'learn by rote' education system means that young employees are unable to take initiatives and develop solutions, relying on clear instructions to follow. This is also true of many of the higher education institutions, even those offering post-graduate courses.

(British expatriate, 50–54 years old, *Automotive, Retail, Construction, and Heavy Equipment*)

The main difference is common sense and logical thinking, we Dutch are educated to think, the Thais are educated to remember.

(Dutch expatriate, 60 or over years old, Tourism)

NON-CONFRONTATIONALITY

Another major characteristic mentioned by the expatriates was the Thais' non-confrontational trait. This is considered to mainly be the result of *Kreng Jai* (เกรงใจ) which is part of Thai cultural values and refers to 'the desire to be self-effacing, respectful, humble and considerate; the wish to avoid embarrassing others' (Siengthai & Vadhanasindhu, 1991: 234). *Kreng Jai* makes the Thais very friendly, warm-hearted, non-confrontational and very considerate about what they say to other people. They tend to say only nice things, not to criticize others directly, and avoid causing others to feel uncomfortable or lose face. They rarely impose on or interrupt others, put forward their comments, wishes, or disagreements—especially to their superiors—or show negative feelings such as anxiety, resentment, and anger (Pornpitakpan, 2000). Several expatriates observed that the Thais were less confrontational than their own home country compatriots. A French expatriate said,

> *In Thailand, it is critical to avoid being critical of people. Thai people do not like conflict, and will do almost anything to avoid conflict in most situations [...] If you compare to European culture, you see here more respect for hierarchy, no confrontation of ideas and people playing more in the comfort zone and status quo rather than challenging current practices.*
> (French expatriate, 45-49 years old, Pharmaceuticals)

It was suggested by some of the expatriate managers that personal confrontations should be kept at a minimum and should always take place behind closed doors, with only the people directly involved present, to prevent anyone from "losing face". This non-confrontational trait was seen by many of the expatriates as an obstacle to reaching the best decisions. One American expatriate commented:

> *I don't like how they never dare to challenge authority. You don't always know their perspectives and opinions. I wish they could put all the ideas on the table and be more open. There's this culture of non-confrontation. You make better decisions [...] if people express [themselves] more. People try to avoid conflict and we don't come to the best decisions.*
> (American expatriate, 35-39 years old, Oil and Gas sector)

A British expatriate expressed the same view, stating:

> *There is no culture of confrontation; so, expressing contrary opinions to a member of the group, especially if that member is older, is very rare. This means that ideas are not fully challenged, and substandard decisions can be taken.*
> (British expatriate, 45-49 years old, Branding Agency)

Many expatriates thought that it would save time and be beneficial if the Thais were more direct, open, assertive and forthcoming, and did not believe it was offensive to express critical views.

In addition to the abovementioned five major characteristics, some of the expatriates also mentioned that, compared to those in their home countries, Thai employees are more shy, sensitive, emotional, indirect, and inwards looking (i.e. lacking global perspective); less ambitious and career minded; they take their work less seriously; prefer a family atmosphere in the workplace and a paternalistic management style; dislike standing out; and dislike taking responsibility in order to avoid the possibility of blame.

Notwithstanding the views expressed above, the expatriates praised their Thai employees for their good work ethics, kindness, friendliness, modesty, loyalty, and for being hard working, intelligent, and helpful.

On the whole, I found that the expatriate leaders had very similar views on the characteristics of Thai employees. The next chapter reports my findings on the patterns by which the 178 expatriate senior managers adjusted to their Thai employees' characteristics.

Chapter Six Executive Summary
Characteristics of Thai employees

- This chapter presents five main values held by and characteristics of Thai employees from the perspectives of the 178 expatriates.

- Over 90% of the expatriates said that leading Thai subordinates was very different from leading their counterparts in their home countries, and that Thai employees featured a number of unique characteristics that had a great influence on the way they had to lead/manage them. The five characteristics most mentioned by the expatriates and how they presented challenges for the expatriates are summarised below:

  - **Inexpressiveness:** The expatriates said Thai employees were inexpressive, unwilling to speak their minds, and tended to keep things to themselves. This inexpressiveness was thought to be the result of a combination of hierarchy, religious beliefs and face-saving. This characteristic presented a challenge for the expatriates as they were unable to understand the viewpoints of their subordinates and the reasoning behind the Thai managers' decisions.

  - **Respect for Seniority and Hierarchy:** The expatriates observed that their Thai employees were very respectful towards older people and people higher up in the organisational hierarchy. The Thai employees' respect for seniority and hierarchy, however, posed several challenges for the expatiates, including: 1) seniority being seen as more important than competency and performance when it came to performance appraisal and promotion; 2) the difficulty for competent younger Thai employees to manage or supervise older colleagues and progress in their careers; 3) the fact that Thai employees hardly ever expressed their views or challenged their superiors, which was an inhibiting factor towards the sharing of ideas and communicating; and 4) the tendency of Thai employees to scrupulously follow their superiors' instructions while seldom questioning or challenging them.

  - **The Great Importance of Saving Face:**
  Many expatriates said that their Thai employees saw 'face' as something that was extremely important to uphold and

that this was one of the key issues faced in leading them. It was a key issue because, for example: Thai staff could have resigned had they lost face; saving face could take priority over team and company interests; and Thai employees tended not to speak in meetings to avoid saying anything that would cause them to lose face.

- o **Limited Initiative and Analytical Ability:** Many expatriates stated that most of their Thai employees expected to be given detailed instructions as to how to complete a task and that most of them lacked the ability to analyse issues. This had been a challenge for the expatriate leaders as they had to provide complete instructions, encourage their Thai staff to take initiatives and responsibilities, and come up with solutions themselves.

- o **Non-confrontationality:** Several expatriates observed that their Thai employees were less confrontational than their own home country counterparts. Thais are very considerate about what they say to other people; they tend to say only nice things, not to criticize others directly, and rarely impose on or interrupt others and put forward their comments and disagreements. This non-confrontational trait was seen by many of the expatriates as an obstacle to making the best decisions; they thought that it would save time and be beneficial if the Thais were more direct, open, assertive, and forthcoming, and did not believe that expressing critical views was offensive.

- In spite of the views expressed above, the expatriates praised their Thai employees for their good work ethics, kindness, friendliness, modesty, loyalty, and for being hard working, intelligent, and helpful.

CHAPTER 7. MODES OF CROSS-CULTURAL LEADERSHIP ADJUSTMENT

This chapter presents my findings on the expatriate managers' modes of cross-cultural leadership adjustment (CLA). In my study, 'modes' of CLA refers to the 'patterns' by which expatriate managers adjust when working in foreign cultural contexts. Exploring these modes will help us understand how expatriate managers adjust in such settings.

I focus on two dimensions of adjustment: the first is the extent to which leaders change their own leadership approaches; the second is the extent to which leaders change their subordinates. The expatriates' modes of adjustment were analysed using the expatriates' responses to two questions 'Do you have to adjust your leadership approach working in Thailand at all?' and 'Have you changed (or tried to change) Thai employees and/or the subsidiary's work practices?'. I used a 7-point Likert scale (1=very little support; 7= very strong support) to rate the expatriates' degrees of adjustment in the two dimensions—leadership adjustment and subordinate change—and then placed the results in a 2x2 matrix as shown below. The framework is adapted from Nicholson's theory of work role transition (Nicholson, 1984).

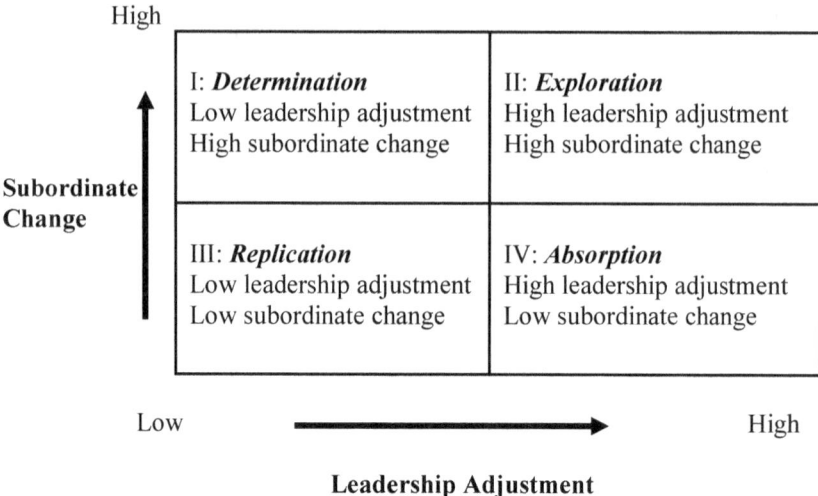

High

| I: *Determination*
 Low leadership adjustment
 High subordinate change | II: *Exploration*
 High leadership adjustment
 High subordinate change |
| III: *Replication*
 Low leadership adjustment
 Low subordinate change | IV: *Absorption*
 High leadership adjustment
 Low subordinate change |

Subordinate Change

Low   High

Leadership Adjustment

The four quadrants indicate different modes of adjustment.

- **Determination** (quadrant I) -- this mode is shown when expatriate leaders actively change their subordinates but make little leadership adjustment.

- **Exploration** (quadrant II) -- it is shown when expatriate leaders significantly change both their leadership approaches and their subordinates.

- **Replication** (quadrant III) -- this mode is shown when expatriate leaders make few leadership adjustments and make little change to their subordinates.

- **Absorption** (quadrant IV) -- this is shown when expatriate leaders modify their leadership approaches but make few changes to their subordinates.

My results show that the expatriate leaders demonstrated three different modes of adjustment: 1) 141 (79.2 %) expatriate managers, and indeed the over-riding majority, displayed the *exploration* mode of adjustment (i.e., they made adjustment to both their leadership approaches and to their subordinates); 2) 20 (11.2 %) displayed the *determination* mode (i.e., they made little adjustment to their leadership approaches but actively tried to change Thai employees and their work practices); and 3) 17 (9.6 %) displayed the *absorption* mode (i.e., they largely adjusted their leadership approaches but not their subordinates). Figure 6 shows the proportions by which the expatriates demonstrated each of the three modes of adjustment. Table 2 presents the three modes of adjustment and the expatriates' nationalities. The following sub-sections provide details for the three modes of adjustment.

Figure 6. Modes of cross-cultural leadership adjustment

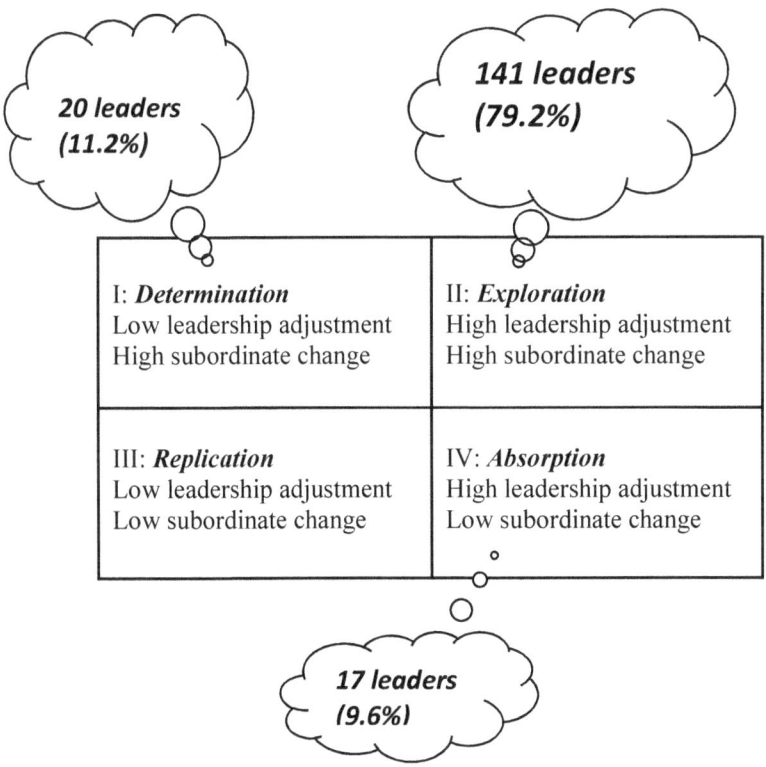

Table 2. Modes of cross-cultural leadership adjustment

| | Modes of CLA (N=178) | | | | | |
| | Exploration | | Determination | | Absorption | |
Nationality	No. of expatriate	(%)	No. of expatriate	(%)	No. of expatriate	(%)
American	17	(9.6)	6	(3.4)	2	(1.1)
Armenian	1	(0.6)	0		0	
Australian	19	(10.7)	1	(0.6)	1	(0.6)
Austria	1	(0.6)	0		0	
Belgian	2	(1.1)	1	(0.6)	0	
British	38	(21.4)	3	(1.7)	11	(6.2)
Canadian	0		1	(0.6)	0	
Danish	2	(1.1)	0		0	
Dutch	11	(6.2)	1	(0.6)	1	(0.6)
French	14	(9.6)	0		1	(0.6)
French and Canadian	1	(0.6)	0		0	
German	12	(6.7)	1	(0.6)	0	
Greek	1	(0.6)	0		0	
Indian	5	(2.8)	0		0	
Irish	2	(1.1)	0		0	
Israeli	1	(0.6)	0		0	
Italian	1	(0.6)	0		0	
Japanese	0		4	(2.2)	0	
Malaysian	2	(1.1)	0		0	
New Zealander	3	(1.7)	0		1	(0.6)
Norwegian	2	(1.1)	0		0	
Pakistani	1	(0.6)	0		0	
Sri Lankan	1	(0.6)	0		0	
Swiss	3	(1.7)	2	(1.1)	0	
Swiss and Danish	1	(0.6)	0		0	
Total	141	(79.2%)	20	(11.2%)	17	(9.6%)

Notes:
Exploration: high leadership adjustment, high subordinate change
Determination: low leadership adjustment, high subordinate change
Absorption: high leadership adjustment, low subordinate change

EXPLORATION MODE OF ADJUSTMENT (high leadership adjustment, high subordinate change)

My research showed that the 141 expatriates adjusted their leadership approaches *and* tried to change their Thai employees because they felt that both these strategies were needed. For example, two British expatriates did so in order to, on the one hand, cater to the characteristics of their Thai subordinates and, on the other hand, improve work efficiency. They stated:

> *'I choose to adjust my approach [...] I focus more on social harmony and not upsetting or offending people. I have a less direct approach in Thailand [...] I have tried to change employees. I encourage them to challenge the status quo, to not be afraid to try new things, and to look at things differently'.*
> (British expatriate, 45-49 years old, Banking)

> *I adjust my style to a more diplomatic one; namely, approaching every level of the organization with respect and yet portraying a "Fatherly" figure, using my age seniority to my advantage. This is required to get engagement and the best out of my staff [...] I have introduced information exchange fora (Town hall meetings); initially, they were unsuccessful, being only one way, but, eventually, when the staff gained more confidence, they became two way. This was needed because of the "information silos" [way in which the company worked], no knowledge was being shared and the company suffered accordingly.*
> (British expatriate, 55-59 years old, Transportation)

The British expatriate's adjustment from a managerial role to a father figure one was made to match the expectation of the Thai subordinates; as observed by Warner (2003: 234), 'the ideal Thai leader is seen as more of a benevolent father than an autocrat'.

A senior manager from Pakistan expressed that he had to change his approach to adjust to the local environment and had tried to make Thai employees more confident in expressing different opinions. He said:

> *Having worked in North America, Europe and the Middle East, adjusting to the Thai environment meant toning down my relatively bold body language and loud verbal expression to match the gentle demeanor of my Thai colleagues. There was also [a] need to pull back on direct criticism and replace it with more indirect 'advice'. [...] I've had to work on building up people's confidence to express dissent.*
> (Pakistan expatriate, 50-54 years old, Research center)

Similarly, an expatriate from Norway also changed his approach to cater to local conditions besides trying to change his Thai subordinates. He said:

> *In Norway, the leader does not get involved in the employees' private lives or care about their families; but here you should if you want them to feel that you care and if you want them to give their best to you and your corporation. You need to be much more soft in the way you talk to or approach your staff, managers. [...] My goal is not to do it my way, but to get the results. If I can get the results by changing my way of leading, or doing things, so be it. [...] I worked on raising their level of self-confidence and helping them see that they were a real valuable asset to the company and that the company really needed, and valued, their input and ideas.*
>
> (Norwegian expatriate, 60 or over years old,
> Coaching - Corporate Training)

An American expatriate said that she tried to change Thai employees while, at the same time, bringing in her own management style and tweaking it to make it work in the Thai culture. For example, she told her subordinates that she expected them to challenge her opinions and decisions (a Western managerial approach), but she also catered for the characteristics of her Thai staff members by demonstrating more care and kindness when leading them. She observed that Thai employees were very conscious of someone exhibiting '*Jai dee*' (good-heartedness, kindness), and were much more committed to the individual and organization if they felt that the leader was kind and genuine and cared about them.

Many of the expatriates perceived that it was important to respect Thai culture and align their approaches with local practices. They not only adjusted their approaches but also tried to inspire and encourage their Thai subordinates to take initiatives and to be more expressive. Two of the expatriates said:

> *For sure, adaptation is required, as we need to respect Thai culture and behaviours. I practise more listening skills, clarify better what the expectations are. Put people at ease through a friendly approach and sense of humour. [...] I try to encourage initiatives and the sharing of ideas. I make it clear that all ideas are good, I choose less stressful environments than meeting rooms: Starbucks, or over lunch. I reward those who bring new*

perspectives or, even better, those who challenge my opinion for the benefit of the business.
                        (French expatriate, 45-49 years old, Pharma)

Yes you have to adjust. Respect for the local culture is important. As a white man you are a Falang (Foreigner) and this role comes with expectations and also some tolerance for not knowing local traditions. [...] I have changed in the way I motivate or manage people in the way I communicate with them. [...] You have to inspire the people to do something and a 'telling' style does not work too well. [...] Thais are very forgiving but, at a certain stage, if they feel it's enough, they can also get aggressive or just leave.
                   (German expatriate, 40-44 years old, Hospitality)

An expatriate from the Netherlands had to adjust his management approach and became less formal and strict to cater to local practices; at the same time, he tried to close the cultural gap. He said:

I have adjusted in terms of [being] less formal and strict as we have to manage business and the sanuk [สนุก, which means to have fun] factor. I learned the hard way following the western approach and being suddenly confronted with resignations as there was too much pressure [...] I try to change work behaviours step by step bringing east to west and west to east to create a better understanding. I setup a programme for training in Europe as well as for Europeans come down to Thailand for some months. This closes the work culture gap a little[...]
                (Dutch expatriate, 45-49 years old, Manufacturing)

Overall, the expatriates displayed the *exploration* mode of adjustment because, on the one hand, they observed that their Thai employees had different characteristics from those found in their home country and in other countries they had worked in, and, on the other hand, they perceived that it was necessary to change their subordinates' characteristics (e.g. make them more expressive). Therefore, they simultaneously adjusted their leadership approaches (e.g., adopting a less direct and more diplomatic approach) and tried to change their Thai staff (e.g., encouraging them to be more expressive) in order to meet the local conditions and to match their personal requirements.

DETERMINATION MODE OF ADJUSTMENT (low leadership adjustment, high subordinate change)

A combination of three key reasons was found to have led 20 expatriates to change their subordinates while maintaining their leadership approaches. First, over half of them believed that the managerial approaches found in their home country were good ways of working and should be used in the Thai subsidiaries. For instance, the four Japanese expatriates regarded teaching Thais Japanese ways of working as vital for the success of their organizations. Two of them stated:

> *Charisma is not necessarily important in leadership. We teach the Thais the "Yamaha style", the way we work.*
> (Japanese expatriate, 35-39 years old, Automotive Manufacturer)

> *I will let them grow within the organization through motivating, teaching, coaching [...] I teach them how to win the negotiation, how to read people's minds, so leadership has to be independent and proactive.*
> (Japanese expatriate, 45-49 years old, Real Estate sector)

An American executive said that he largely maintained his American managerial approach and that this was more forceful than that normally found in Thailand:

> *I would say that my style is much more forceful in terms of responsibility, accountability, straight line, whereas, in the Thai culture, things are looser.*
> (American expatriate, 55-59 years old, Banking sector)

Second, five of the expatriates maintained their leadership approaches because they perceived that it was effective in any multicultural context. For example, the Canadian expatriate (45-49 years old, Banking) said that he only needed to make few adjustments, as his leadership 'is one that has already been used for decades in multicultural groups and has proven to be very effective globally'.

Third, most of the expatriates believed that their Thai employees and the hierarchical system of Thai organizations needed to be changed. They tried to use what they believed to be good ways of working. Instead of adjusting their leadership approaches to accommodate the characteristics of their subordinates, they tried to change the status quo. To do so, they encouraged their subordinates to challenge opinions, the chain of command and decisions. In addition, they tried to establish an environment in which employees felt comfortable enough to express their views and break down factors, such as hierarchy, that could hinder teamwork and the expression of good ideas. A Japanese executive said:

> *I'm trying to create an atmosphere so that there's no high wall between my staff and me. I'm trying to make the atmosphere like we are family here. I'm trying to go to see the [real estate] sites with my staff and work with them directly so that there is no hierarchy.*
>
> (Japanese expatriate, 45-49 years old, Real Estate sector)

Taken together, these expatriates maintained their leadership approaches and actively tried to change their subordinates because they perceived their approach to be an effective way of leading people and because they perceived it was necessary to change local employees and work practices. In other words, they tried to change their staff in order to match their personal requirements.

ABSORPTION MODE OF ADJUSTMENT (high leadership adjustment, low subordinate change)

I found that 17 expatriates did not try to change their subordinates but adjusted their own leadership approaches because they observed that, culturally, the Thais behaved differently in the workplace and they concluded that they had to use different leadership approaches. For example, one British executive said that he had to be gentler and more patient, and give more encouragement. Another British expatriate said that he had adjusted his approach, but had not tried to change his Thai subordinates. He said:

> *I basically have become a passive helper/critic. I even give advice in a very passive way so that [my] staff doesn't lose face. I don't believe this is a good way of doing things, but the Thai ego in the workplace is easily bruised [...] I only give advice. In the end, employees are either good at their jobs or they are not. If the latter, then they usually don't last long.*
>
> (British expatriate, 40-44 years old, Media sector)

To understand their subordinates' viewpoints while fulfilling the needs of the Thais to 'hide collectively' by giving 'group' opinions rather than individual ones, the expatriates sought unspoken views through indirect means; for example, getting anonymous input in group settings or via supervisors, or talking to staff unofficially during lunch breaks. One executive stated that, in order to draw out information, opinions and recommendations, he had asked questions such as 'What would you do?', 'What have we tried before?', and 'What do you recommend we do?' even when he already had an opinion. Although he occasionally got frustrated and had to give his own opinion, he believed that asking questions was the only way to hear his staff's recommendations. He stressed the importance of adjusting to the local environment, stating:

> *The most important thing here is this understanding that, if you are the most senior person, you have to act in a very different way to how you would act in a western environment. Ask more questions, keep your own opinions to yourself or spend more time.*
>
> (British Executive, 50-54 years old, Automotive sector)

Overall, I found that these expatriates adjusted their leadership and made little change to their Thai subordinates mainly because they observed that their Thai employees behaved differently from those in their home countries and thus perceived it to be important to align their leadership approaches with their followers' characteristics, rather than to try and change them. In other words, they adjusted their approach in order to meet the local conditions.

In summary, I found that the characteristics of Thai employees, the hierarchical system and the leaders' perceptions exert a strong influence on the expatriates' modes of adjustment. I also found that *exploration* was the dominant mode of adjustment among the leaders; only small numbers showed the *absorption* and *determination* modes. In other words, most of them simultaneously adjusted their own leadership approach and tried to change Thai employees; a small proportion either adjusted their leadership approaches or actively tried to change their subordinates. In the next chapter, I report the challenges in leading Thai employees as perceived by the expatriates.

Chapter Seven Executive Summary
Modes of Cross-cultural Leadership Adjustment

- This chapter reports my findings on the modes/patterns by which the 178 expatriate senior managers adjusted in responding to their employees' characteristics mentioned in chapter 6. I focussed on two dimensions of adjustment: the first is the extent to which leaders change their own leadership approaches (leadership adjustment); the second is the extent to which leaders attempted to change their subordinates (subordinate change). I analysed the expatriates' modes of adjustment using a 2x2 matrix based on these two dimensions.

- The results show that the expatriate leaders adopted three different modes of adjustment, with most them simultaneously adjusting their own leadership approach and attempting to change their Thai employees. The three modes of adjustment are:

  1) the **exploration** mode of adjustment: 141 (79.2%) of the expatriate managers—indeed the overriding majority—made adjustments to both their own leadership approaches and to their subordinates;

  2) the **determination** mode of adjustment: 20 (11.2%) of the expatriate managers made little adjustment to their leadership approaches but actively tried to change their Thai employees and their work practices; and

  3) the **absorption** mode of adjustment: 17 (9.6%) of the expatriate managers largely adjusted their leadership approaches but did not try to change their subordinates.

- Those expatriates who displayed the *exploration* mode of adjustment, on the one hand, adjusted their own approaches as they observed that their Thai employees had characteristics that were different from those found in their home countries and in others in which they had worked, and, on the other hand, tried to change their Thai employees' characteristics as they perceived that it was necessary to do so (e.g., to bring them to be more expressive).

- Those expatriates who displayed the *determination* mode of adjustment perceived their approach to be an effective way of leading people and that it was necessary to change local employees and work practices.

55

- Those expatriates who displayed the *absorption* mode of adjustment observed that their Thai employees behaved differently from those in their home countries and thus perceived it to be preferable to align their leadership approaches with their followers' characteristics, rather than to try and change the latter.

CHAPTER 8. CHALLENGES IN LEADING THAI EMPLOYEES

The expatiate leaders indicated that the challenges in leading Thai employees were mainly associated with their characteristics. In this chapter, I report the five challenges most mentioned by the expatriates.

COMMUNICATION AND LANGUAGE BARRIERS

A great number of expatriates pointed out that a major challenge in leading Thai employees is communication. This challenge involves two inter-related aspects, one is the Thai employees' English language fluency and the other is the style of communication found in Thailand.

English language fluency   Many expatriates pointed out that language was the biggest challenge for them and that the language barrier is one of the most difficult challenges to overcome. This is because all documents related to government/local authorities are in Thai, over 90% of government officials don't speak English, and the average Thai employee's grasp of the English language is lower than that found in other Asian countries in which they had worked. An expatriate from New Zealand said,

> The other obvious problem is the language barrier, both written and spoken. I have worked with my team for nearly nine years and they still state that they only understand 60% of what I say at times.
>
> (New Zealander Executive, 50–54 years old, Construction Project Management)

An Australian expatriate said,

> [it is] often stated that Thai's 'listen to but do not hear' what is being said – they switch off when there is [a continuous stream

of] spoken words. Communication therefore needs to be very visual [...] whiteboard and rudimentary flow charts are used to convey understanding and logic.
(Australian expatriate, 60 or over years old,
Logistics & Transport Services)

An American expatriate expressed that Thailand is a more difficult work location due to the language. English is his company's official language, but is not well spoken at the Thai subsidiary, especially the lower in the organization he goes. Some expatriates criticised the fact that English is very poorly taught in Thai public schools, which leads to the majority of Thais having a very low mastery of English.

As a matter of fact, communicating in a different language and getting the message across is challenging for both sides – the expatriates and their Thai employees. In most situations, the expatriate managers cannot effectively communicate in Thai, while the locals, although they do have some ability to communicate in English, do not have the depth of vocabulary to understand it in detail.

The low English language fluency had led to a number of management issues. For example, it had led to delays and errors in the employees' work, as they simply were not carrying out the tasks required because they didn't understand what was being asked of them, or they misinterpreted instructions but had gone ahead without questioning. It had also caused negative feelings among Thai employees. A British expatriate shared his experience in dealing with staff difficulties caused by poor communication and language fluency:

I had to work on communication between some group members as their English was poor and my Thai wasn't sufficient to solve the problem. The group could become very frustrated through not understanding completely or, more commonly, believing they had understood and thinking poorly about the decision, causing anger that played out over all work tasks; they became very difficult to deal with.
(British expatriate, 40–44 years old, Public Relations)

In addition, the lack of a good grasp of English had made it even more difficult for Thai employees to air their opinions, which intensified their inexpressiveness, as they thought that speaking poor or incorrect English was embarrassing and conducive to loosing face.

A British expatriate, who had worked in Thailand for over 18 years, observed that the Thai employees' English had improved, but commented that 'there is still a long way to go'. A Malaysian expatriate commented that 'there needs to be a revamp of the whole education system in the country at the grassroots-levels'.

Communication style In addition to the varying degrees of fluency in the English language, communication is a challenge because the styles of social language and communication are different in Thailand. They vary by age, gender, relative rank, and closeness between the speaker and the listener. For example, women often end a sentence with *kha* and men with *khrap* for politeness (Pornpitakpan, 2000).

Some expatriates indicated that several points of communication etiquette are associated with the Thai language and culture. They suggested that a speaker communicating in English must be aware of the differences in communication style and apply the Thai rules of etiquette. For example, one of the key differences in communication concerns pitch and volume; in Thailand, a person that speaks loudly is sending the message that he or she is angry. Speaking softly is a necessity which shows politeness and respectfulness. Another example being the Thai employees' propensity to say 'yes' or nodding their heads during face-to-face communication; this, however, does not mean they have understood or agreed. Some expatriates thought that this 'yes mantra' may have resulted from cultural factors such as the importance of maintaining harmonious relationships, showing politeness, and avoiding the risk of losing face. An American expatriate advised that constant mindfulness of the uniqueness of Thai culture is required when communicating and articulating ideas, objectives, criticism, and performance criteria.

SHORT SUPPLY OF TALENTS AND HIGH EMPLOYEE TURNOVER

Another most mentioned challenge was the shortage of competent employees and high employee turnover rate.

Shortage of Talent Several expatriates from the high-tech, telecom and banking industries indicated that there was a short supply of talent in their industries. For example, a French expatriate from the telecom industry said that a Thai employee with international management skills will cost the same as an expatriate because the demand for employees with such skills is a lot higher than the supply. Finding good and qualified employees does not seem to be limited to the aforementioned industries. An expatriate from the hospitality sector observed that some industries in Thailand are 'employee markets' in which employers not only struggle to find qualified employees, but there is a shortage altogether.

Some expatriates attributed the skill gaps to the Thai educational curriculum and system. They criticised it in that it had not kept up with the swift business development in other parts of the world. They indicated that, compared to their counterparts in other countries, local Thai graduates have less knowledge and experience. The skill gaps made it necessary to invest time in coaching and money in employee training in order to improve staff skills and knowledge. Coaching, however, could represent another challenge when the language barrier is in the equation. As an Australian expatriate said,

> Admittedly, I am very lucky and have a very competent team in general; but, when I have the odd person who is not as skilled as the rest of the team and then you throw in a language barrier into the mix, I do find it a lot more challenging to coach through the skill gap.
>
> (Australian expatriate, 35–39 years old, Hospitality)

High turnover rate For many expatriates, due to the high employee turnover rate, investing in employee training could be a risky undertaking for a business. Several expatriates identified employee retention as a big challenge, as employees could easily resign and move on to new opportunities. They are able to do so as the unemployment rate is very low in Thailand (the average unemployment rate from 2001 to 2015 was 1.52 %; it was less than 1% at the time the research was conducted). A French expatriate said,

> The main challenge is to keep the good employees working with you. There is such a turnover that you can [very easily] lose the team you tried to set up.
>
> (French expatriate, 40–44 years old, IT development)

Many expatriates said that their employees may resign in situations such as: 'if a boss upsets them even a little', 'if they feel they are misunderstood or mistreated', 'if they do not get along with their manager', and 'if you tell them they did something wrong'. They said that employees can decide to leave the company 'the next day' or 'without any notice'. Several expatriates expressed that the Thai employees' tolerance towards critical or negative feedback is very low, and criticism can easily contribute to employee turnover. Two of them said:

Thais do not easily accept corrective criticism, especially if they are older than their direct manager. It is a challenge and requires some management innovation to build awareness connected with what is expected pertaining to personal performance, following protocol, etc.

(American expatriate, 55–59 years old, IT, Food & Beverage)

Pride is also a big thing, you can tell someone off in NZ [New Zealand] and you both get over it and move on, Thais take it to heart and will [sometimes] resign if they think they have done wrong.

(New Zealander expatriate, 50–54 years old, Construction Project Management)

A British expatriate described how trying to retain staff is like walking on eggshells:

It's very hard to criticise Thai staff, and I find [that], much of the time, if you don't walk on eggshells, you will lose staff. This is challenging.

(British expatriate, 40–44 years old, Media)

Overall, many expatriates saw employee retention as a big challenge and indicated that the high turnover rate had a negative effect on employee discipline, motivation and commitment.

LOWER SENSE OF OWNERSHIP AND ACCOUNTABILITY

Another frequently mentioned challenge was related to the Thai employees' sense of ownership and accountability. Giving workers job ownership and putting them in charge of how they do their job is advocated by workplace psychologists as a way to promote well-being at work, as the sense of ownership provides an individual with a sense of purpose in one's job and a feeling of accomplishment. However, according to the expatriates, the concepts of sense of ownership and accountability are not very developed in the Thai workplace. Many expatriates pointed out that Thai employees are less independent and proactive and do not often take initiatives and responsibility. For the expatriates, the challenge is getting staff to be brave enough to take initiatives, think for themselves, make decisions and be accountable. Two expatriates said,

The main challenge is to empower people to think and decide for themselves and not automatically follow the hierarchy.

(Dutch expatriate, 40–44 years old, Telecom)

Challenges were people always looking upwards for answers
and leadership rather than to themselves
(British expatriate, 55–59 years old, Manufacturing)

The hierarchy system in Thai society and workplace is thought to have a great influence on this. Thai employees are seldom empowered to make decisions and take responsibilities; they are expected to follow the instructions given by their superiors. Due to this hierarchical tradition, Thai employees are accustomed to following instructions and are not confident in performing a task on their own, without advice from their supervisors. As a result, many expatiates stated that Thai employees need to be given specific instructions or directions as to how to complete their tasks. Micro management, rather than outcome management, and constant monitoring are thus seen as a necessity when leading/managing Thai employees.

In addition to hierarchy, the issue of 'face' is thought to also play a part. Many expatriates observed that Thai employees were unwilling to take responsibilities as they wanted to avoid being blamed for mistakes, which would lead them to lose face. A British expatriate said,

> *In our organisation, Thai employees had not previously been empowered to make decisions on their own. It is a challenge to change this behaviour, due to the fear of making mistakes and suffering the consequences [...] ensure you get the most of their good ideas, encouraging them to challenge the status quo without exposing themselves and losing face.*
> (British expatriate, 55–59 years old, Transportation)

CULTURAL DIFFERENCES AND SELF-ADJUSTMENT

Another key challenge for the expatriates was to understand and adapt to Thai culture. Many expatriates expressed that Thai cultural values – based around *Kreng Jai*, 'face', respect for seniors, and a mentality of conflict avoidance – were very different from their own cultures and beliefs. Thus, a key challenge was learning about Thai culture and adjusting to the local culture. The two most mentioned adjustments they had needed to make or had made were being *indirect* and *patient*.

A great number of the expatriates mentioned that one of adjustments they had made or needed to make was to be 'indirect' in order to avoid causing offence to their Thai staff. They said that most Thai employees would not easily accept corrective criticism, especially if they were older than their direct manager, and that they would be easily offended if they were told they had done something wrong. The following quotes illustrate why being indirect is necessary in Thailand:

> *In my home country, it is possible to be direct without causing offence (when acting sensibly), but, in Thailand, there is a good chance [that] such a 'direct' approach would cause some form of offence or resentment and, as such, be counter-productive.*
> (Australian expatriate, 55–59 years old, Financial Services)

> *The challenge is to find a way of pointing out [any] right and wrong doings without insulting or offending them. I have seen employees just leave and never come back after being told that they had made a really big mistake.*
> (German expatriate, 50–54 years old, IT Services)

> *We have to be careful in [how we] behave with our local counterparts. The Thai way [requires us not to] say things in a too straightforward manner [...] but, rather, [to drop hints] so that the other party will understand what we have in mind. It is time consuming but it is part of a process to get along with the local people.*
> (French expatriate, 45–49 years old, Telecom)

> *Sometimes [it is] difficult to get straight to the point of an issue, [we] must set the scene, make the individual comfortable with the topic and then try and get the point [across] without causing upset or loss of face over the 'offending' topic. In my country, it's fine to be direct about an issue in the work place and it is not considered confrontational.*
> (British expatriate, 50–54 years old, Hospitality)

Some expatriates said that many Thai employees took any feedback and comments given to them as personal criticism; as a consequence, the feedback was not communicated further or handled appropriately.

They suggested that, to be effective and avoid causing offence, expatriate leaders must minimise direct confrontations, especially in the presence of other people; that expressing disagreements should always be done one-to-one and not in the presence of a big audience; and more subtly, speaking in a calm voice and ensuring that the Thai staff did not get upset even under deadline or other work related stress.

Another key adjustment made by many expatriates was to be much more patient and to learn to approach issues and resolve them over time. Patience was needed in several occasions. For example, the expatriates said that it took time to develop the staff's work practices, such as making quick decisions and taking responsibilities; it took time 'to explain how the steps fit into the rulebook of their minds, as speed is not one of the virtues'; it took time to draw out the viewpoints of their Thai employees; and it took time for the Thai staff to accept and make changes—all of which required patience. The expatriates indicated that, although it took more time to get things done, with patience, things were eventually delivered. Some expatriates said that they had adjusted by taking their time and not pushing their teams too hard, as doing this too often had led to resistance and had had a negative effect on their work. An Australian expatriate stated:

> *Patience is an essential ingredient in Thailand. What may take just one meeting in the West can take two or three weeks for people to come to terms with and accept. If you push too hard, you can lose people permanently. Knowing when to push and when to back off is essential.*
>
> (Australian expatriate, 50–54 years old, Technology)

The expatriates said that it was necessary to be culturally sensitive and learn the culture at as many levels as possible. They indicated that there were lots of cultural points that had to be respected. For example, the respect for seniors, the conflict avoidance mentality, saving the other party's 'face' in conflictual situations, and the traditional soft approach of Thai people.

Adjusting to the various aspects of Thai culture and/or ways of doing things proved to be challenging for many expatriates. A French expatriate said that, depending on the individuals, it could be difficult for westerners to adjust; he stated that 'few really succeed and many give up and quit'.

Some expatriates, nevertheless, tried to learn to work within the cultural and societal expectations, as they observed that western methods rarely worked without modification. An American expatriate said that it took time to adjust but that, once he had understood the cultural differences and the Thai ways of doing things, it was 'not difficult to adjust to this lovely and polite society'. A British expatriate said that it was important to understand Thai cultural values; he made sure there was a cultural fit in the workplace:

> *My number one goal is to have a happy team ([which] means*

64

high staff retention) so I ensure that the office atmosphere is a cultural fit; i.e. not imposing western values on the office although it is a western company. [...] [In my office,] I have a picture of the King [and one of the] Buddha, I buy flowers for the Buddha [and] go to the temple with my team...

(British expatriate, 40–44 years old, Market Research and Marketing Recruitment)

RESISTANCE TO CHANGE AND SLOW ACCEPTANCE OF CHANGE

Implementing and managing change are among the items on the business leaders' list of key tasks. Like those in other parts of the world, most Thai employees dislike change, but some expatriates said that resistance to change is stronger among Thais. Several expatriates perceived that Thais resist changes mainly because, at the individual level, they 'prefer consistency or routine, day in day out', 'tend to feel that their way is the right way (particularly for staff at the professional level) and 'would rather stay in a situation in which they can be quiet and less disturbed'. At the national level, the expatriates regarded the relaxed and introspective national culture as being responsible for the employees' unwillingness to accept change. Two expatriates stated:

Thais are not very eager to change things; their relaxed culture makes it hard for them to focus on change as a good thing, why work extra to do this differently if it's working well under their eyes?

(Italian expatriate, 35–39 years old, IT/e-commerce)

Whereas Western employees aspire to achieve higher levels of leadership, responsibility, and status as a manager, Thais, in large numbers, seek to find a balance where they are earning enough for their life expectations and then seek to avoid being pushed higher [...] Thais, as a nation, are more introspective. They focus, as a benchmark, on what happens within Thailand, rather than measuring themselves against other SE Asian or global best practices. All these attributes make it challenging to motivate, drive change [...]

(Australian expatriate, 50–54 years old, Technology)

A number of expatriates indicated that the biggest challenge was to get their staff to accept any necessary changes and getting over the initial hurdle/inertia. They said the biggest issue was to sell the need for change, explain why it was important and why it really could mean something for all of them. A change could be difficult to implement if it fell out of the staff's comfort zone.

Some expatriates said that some changes were eventually implemented once the staff had realised that they were necessary, although this took quite a long time to sink in. The challenge presented by the employees' resistance to change didn't end there; the expatriates said that their next and ongoing challenge was maintaining change and making sure that everything was going well:

> *The ongoing challenge is always to prevent them [from] falling back to the 'this is how we do it in Thailand' excuse for not being bothered to do it right.*
>
> (British expatriate, 45–49 years old, Engineering)

Chapter Eight Executive Summary
Challenges in leading Thai employees

- This chapter presents the five main challenges most mentioned by the 178 expatriates in leading their Thai employees.

- These are:

  - **Communication and language barriers:** this challenge involves two inter-related aspects; one is the varying degree of the Thai employees' English language fluency. Many expatriates pointed out that the average Thai employee's grasp of the English language was lower than that found in other Asian countries in which they had worked. Such low English language fluency had led to a number of management issues; for example, it had led to delays and errors in the employees' work, as they didn't understand what was being asked of them or they misinterpreted instructions. The other aspect involved the styles of communication and social language which varied by age, gender, relative rank, and closeness between the speaker and the listener. The expatriates suggested that a speaker communicating in English should be aware of the differences in communication styles and apply the Thai rules of etiquette.

  - **Short supply of talents and high employee turnover:** there was a short supply of talent in some industries in Thailand; thus, finding qualified employees was challenging. Some expatriates commented that, compared to their counterparts in other countries, local Thai graduates had less knowledge and experience. This made it necessary to invest time in coaching and money in training in order to bridge the employee skills and knowledge gaps. Many expatriates saw employee retention as a big challenge as their Thai employees' would resign without any notice over situations such as: "if a boss upsets them even a little" and "if they feel they are misunderstood or mistreated". The expatriates indicated that the high turnover rate had a negative effect on employee discipline, motivation, and commitment.

  - **Lower sense of ownership and accountability:** Many expatriates said that a sense of ownership and accountability was not very developed in the Thai workplace and pointed out that Thai employees were less independent and proactive and did not often take initiatives and responsibility. The challenge faced by the expatriates was finding ways to encourage their staff members to be brave enough to take initiatives, think for themselves, make decisions, and be accountable.

- o **Cultural differences and self-adjustment:** Adjusting to the various aspects of Thai culture and/or ways of doing things proved to be challenging for many expatriates. They said that Thai cultural values—based as they were around *Kreng Jai*, 'face', respect for seniors, and a mentality of conflict avoidance—were very different from their own. The two most mentioned adjustments they had needed to make or had made involved being *indirect* and *patient*. Indirectness in communication was needed as most Thai employees would not easily accept corrective criticism and would easily become offended if they were told they had done something wrong. Patience was needed as they had to spend more time to, for example, develop their Thai employees' work practices, explain their tasks, and draw out their viewpoints.

- o **Resistance to and slow acceptance of change:** Like their counterparts in other parts of the world, most Thai employees disliked change; however, some expatriates said that resistance to change was stronger among Thais. The expatriates perceived that their employees resisted changes mainly because consistency or routine characterised the preferred way of working and the relaxed and introspective national culture had led the employees to be unwilling to accept change.

PART IV.
SUGGESTIONS FROM THE
EXPATRIATE SENIOR
MANAGERS

CHAPTER 9. INSIGHTS AND SUGGESTIONS FOR LEADING THAI EMPLOYEES EFFECTIVELY

This chapter presents the suggestions made by the expatriate leaders for leading Thai employees; where appropriate, the ways in which the leaders adjusted are also reported.

LEARN, BE MINDFUL OF, RESPECT AND ACCEPT SOCIAL AND CULTURAL EXPECTATIONS AND DIFFERENCES

Many leaders stated that Western methods rarely work without modification in Thailand, and suggested that it is important to understand the Thai culture and value system and to learn to work within cultural and societal expectations. They suggested that, in order to work well with Thai staff, expatiate managers should be 'culturally sensitive and respectful', to 'actively listen and tune' and 'adapt to each individual', and to 'learn the culture at as many levels as possible'.

In particular, they emphasised the importance of understanding the following aspects to lead Thai employees:

- the concept of 'face' (see chapter 5 & 6)
- the concept of *Kreng Jai* (see chapter 6)
- the conflict avoidance mentality (see chapter 6)
- the soft approach (see chapter 5)
- the respect for seniors and elders (see chapter 5 & 6)

The expatriates said that it is crucial to understand and respect the cultural and societal norms listed above and how they translate into day-to-day workplace behaviours. Failing to do so will lead to negative consequences, such as difficulties in maintaining relationships with Thai staff, losing the respect of one's team, struggling to manage effectively, facing reductions in productivity and increases in staff turnover.

In addition to understanding the abovementioned aspects, the expatriates said that it is important to let employees know that you respect their culture. An Australian expatriate explained how his effort in trying to understand local practices helped him lead Thai employees:

> I was careful at the start about cultural sensitivities – what to say, what not to say – before I brought my own personality out in full. I asked lots of questions – work, culture and language-related. This seemed to help [me to bond], as the people appreciated that, as a foreigner, I was interested in Thailand and, importantly, its people [...] I used the people in my team and asked them about things before barging in as a foreigner and trying to change things. I asked for their advice on how to approach things.
> (Australian expatriate, 45–49 years old, Hospitality)

Some of the expatriates not only interacted with their Thai staff at work; they also mingled with local people in order to learn the subtleties of the cultural norms. An expatriate from Norway stated:

> I have been here a long time. I think that one thing that really helps is to mingle with the locals, not just the ones who have studied or lived and worked abroad, but to build friendships with local people. It helps you to see them from a whole different perspective than just in the office.
> (Norwegian expatriate, 60 or over years old, Coaching, Corporate Training)

Other expatriates made an effort to learn the upbringing and intentions of their employees to understand their work behaviours. Two expatriates said,

> [...] you have to understand the upbringing of Thais in their families/school/university to understand their reactions. I've started to read Thai mythology and to become more "Thai" in my way of doing things
> (German expatriate, 35–39 years old, Management Consulting)

> I focus more on understanding why people act as they do and try and see intentions rather than just actions.
> (British expatriate, 45–49 years old, Banking)

71

From the above, we can see that understanding Thai values and ways of doing things, and then integrating them into the leadership role requires time, effort and adjustment. Several expatriates expressed that, although they took time, such adjustments were not difficult to make when one understood and respected the local culture. The following statements show how understanding, accepting and respecting the local culture made working with Thai staff an enjoyable experience.

> *It takes time to adjust but, if you understand the cultural differences and study the Thai ways, it is not difficult to adjust to this lovely and polite society.*
> (American expatriate, 45–49 years old, Life Insurance)

> *We enjoy working with Thai nationals and have learned to adapt to the cultural differences.*
> (Austrian expatriate, 50–54 years old, Hospitality)

> *All in all, a delight to work with, if the manager is sensitive to the pride Thais carry with respect to their culture and doing things the Thai way.*
> (Pakistani expatriate, 50–54 years old, Research)

> *You have to guess people's feelings. You sometimes have to accept slow processes. However, it is in fact easy to work with Thai people as long as you accept/respect some cultural differences. And, in the end, Thai people tend to give their time generously.*
> (French expatriate, 60 or over years old, Marketing Research)

ADJUST YOUR OWN EMOTIONS AND BEHAVIOURS

Another key aspect suggested by the expatriates to effectively lead/manage Thai employees is changing one's own emotions and behaviour. Several emotional and behavioural aspects were suggested to be adjusted. Below, I list the key aspects.

Use Indirect Approaches   As illustrated in chapter 8, many expatriates expressed that they had to adjust and adopt a more indirect approach. They suggested that it is necessary to adopt an indirect approach in order to avoid causing offence to Thai employees and trigger emotional reactions in them. Many of the leaders expressed that most Thai employees do not easily accept direct corrective criticism, that they take corrective feedback and comments as personal criticism, and will be offended if they are told in public that they have done something wrong. Some of the expatriates said that they had to change from a direct western approach to an indirect one after experiencing staff resignations as a result of giving direct comments to their subordinates. They recommended the following dos and don'ts:

Dos:

- ✓ Communicate more indirectly.

- ✓ Pull back on direct criticism and replace it with more indirect 'advice'.

- ✓ Always express disagreement one-to-one and not in front of a big audience.

- ✓ Avoid open confrontation at all costs

- ✓ Keep personal confrontations at a minimum and always behind closed doors, in the presence of only those people who are directly involved, to avoid the person losing face.

- ✓ Be more subtle, speak in a calm voice.

- ✓ Focus more on social harmony and avoid upsetting or offending people.

- ✓ Find accommodating, non-confrontational communication methods to gain agreement on objectives, strategies and plan.

- ✓ Say things in a more indirect way, drop hints so that the other party understands what we have in mind.

Don'ts

- × Avoid saying things too directly or in a too straightforward manner – many Thai people feel that they are losing face if you are too direct with them.

- × Don't push for more information to try to reach a conclusion— this will be seen as being too aggressive, and cause other problems at a later time.

- × Avoid being 'open and honest' in communicating, particularly when giving negative feedback.

- × Avoid getting straight to the point of an issue. Set the scene, make the individual comfortable with the topic and then try and get the point across without causing upset or loss of face.

×   Never speak with a strong tone.

×   Don't point.

Be Patient   As also illustrated in chapter 8, many expatriates expressed that they had to adjust to become more patient. They adjusted the level as well as the intensity of their patience; some said that they needed 'a lot more patience' when leading Thai employees, others said that 'patience is required at all times'. Some expatriates expressed that the main adjustment they had made had been in the patience which was required in various occasions, as speedily is not how most of their Thai staff do things. The expatriates said it took longer time to get things done in Thailand; for example, it took longer to develop the staff, to explain work procedures, to get the staff's viewpoints and responses, to gain a mutual understanding and to achieve work targets. They said that, with patience, these things were eventually delivered; by contrast, lacking in patience and pushing Thai employees too hard would lead to resistance.

The expatriates expressed that making adjustments and being more patient is essential in Thailand and suggested the following:

▪   Be patient.

▪   Be more patient.

▪   Learn to be very patient.

    (PS. I listed the same thing three times, not to test your patience, but to illustrate how earnest the expatriate leaders' suggestion was and to underline how important being patient is.)

▪   Learn to slow down and not to react immediately.

▪   Learn to approach and resolve issues over time.

▪   Take your time and do not push too hard.

Stay Calm and Never Lose One's Temper   Thai people value harmonious relationships and are mild/gentle mannered and conflict averse. They abide by the principle of *Jai Yen* (ใจ เย็น) (which is the Thai expression for staying cool and composed, not showing strong emotions, such as anger and frustration, openly) and expect their colleagues and supervisors to do the same. About a fifth of the expatriates expressed that shouting, pointing, yelling and swearing in the Thai workplace will lead to serious negative consequences, such as breakdown in communication, loss of credibility and counter-productivity.

Thus, many expatriates advised that it is very important to stay calm in all situations and at all times and not loose one's temper in front of Thai employees even if serious mistakes had been made. Some expatriates said that remaining calm was challenging for them and they had to come up with different ways to remain calm. For example, a Dutch expatriate said that he 'counted to ten a lot', a French expatriate said that he had to take time and work on himself in order keep calm, and an American expatriate said that he had learnt to tone down his verbal response when he was upset.

Some expatriates said that showing emotion is frowned upon in Thailand and suggested to hide one's emotions, not to lose one's temper, not to raise one's voice, and never show anger, frustration or impatience. Below is the advice given by some of the expatriates:

> *Western staff have to be very careful in their behaviour as becoming angry, shouting etc. are not only frowned upon, but will make [future] working relationships very difficult.*
> (Dutch expatriate, 55–59 years old, Oil and Gas)

> *One has to accept that raised voices, or any other form of overt annoyance will close the door and damage your reputation and relationships [...] further cementing the underlying belief that foreigners are rude and aggressive.*
> (British expatriate, 50–54 years old, Financial Services)

> *If you, as a leader, have an aggressive or overly demanding attitude, make a change. It will be easier for Thais to accept you. They are mild mannered and we need to adjust our way of communication.*
> (Malaysian expatriate, 60 or over years old, Chemicals and Pharmaceuticals)

> *A confrontational, angry, or [loud] style will guarantee failure.*
> (Irish expatriate, 45–49 years old, Supply Chain Management)

An American expatriate from the market research sector said that a creative expatriate colleague of hers freely showed her emotions when upset, stressed, happy, or angry. By doing so, that female colleague had alienated some of her direct employees who did not know how to deal with her emotions. Thai employees expect their leaders to be calm and nice. The key message from the expatriate is that getting angry doesn't improve the situation and that you achieve your outcome or goal a lot quicker by remaining cool and calm.

Adopt a Soft, Harmonious and Relationship-based Approach
Another suggestion made by the expatriates is to adopt a soft, harmonious and relationship-based approach. Several expatriates said that Thais are soft spoken people and consider raised voices equivalent to shouting. Because of that, some expatriates said that they had to tone down their relatively bold body language and loud verbal expressions to match the gentle demeanour of their Thai colleagues. They suggested that, in Thailand, the language used has to be soft and that expatriates must adjust their own style of communication and be constantly aware of the intensity and volume of their voice so that their Thai staff won't feel that they are angry or disapproving.

A Norwegian expatriate who had worked in Thailand for more than 25 years suggested the adoption of a soft approach and said that he had been willing to change his own leadership approach in order to get the results he wanted:

> You need to be much softer in the way you talk to or approach your staff. They easily get sensitive and [clam] up. They won't tell you why, so it is better to just take a [somewhat] softer approach. [...] My goal is not to do it my way, but to get the results. If I can get the results by changing my way of leading or doing things, so be it.
> (Norwegian expatriate, 60 or over years old, Coaching and
> Corporate Training)

Many expatriates said that they found a direct and authoritarian approach to be ineffective, as it can lead to resistance and employee resignations; on the other hand, establishing friendly and harmonious working relationships made things easier as Thai employees value them. Many expatriates said they had made more of an effort to maintain workplace harmony and invested more time in building relationships with their team members in Thailand than in their home countries. To maintain harmonious relationships, they had adopted various measures; for example, some expatriates said they had become less formal and strict and less focused on discipline (e.g., the timing of meetings); they smiled more and used a friendlier and humorous approach to put people at ease. Two expatriates said,

> *I focus more on social harmony and [on] not upsetting or offending people.*
>
> (British expatriate, 45–49 years old, Banking)

> *In the Thai context, social harmony in the organization, for example, may lead to stronger sustained performance in the long term than a short term task oriented result focus.*
>
> (British expatriate, 45–49 years old, Insurance)

Many expatriates emphasised that, to maintain a good working relationship, it is important to have regular social interaction and provide social support. They said that, as Thais are sociable, they spent time socializing with their Thai staff (e.g., talking about family, trips, the journey to work etc.; making jokes with each other; and bringing food for their team) to build and maintain good working relationships. An American expatriate said,

> *Thais are very sociable, and like to have fun in the workplace. Casual conversation and banter helps to strengthen relationships.*
>
> (American expatriate, 40–44 years old, Real Estate)

The expatriates also suggested being more considerate of the emotions and feelings of Thai staff. They observed that Thai people are very sensitive and are more productive when they are happy and comfortable. Some expatriates said that they had to carefully 'read' the expressions of their Thai staff as they rarely express themselves openly. The expatriates warned that, if a leader only focusses on business matters without considering staff emotions, he or she will be faced with 'passive resistance' (i.e., withholding support, ignoring or refusing to follow instructions without using sanctionatory methods) from Thai staff. A British expatriate said,

> *The Thais are proud and generally of a quiet, respectful demeanour - but they can (covertly) adopt a stubborn uncooperative manner if they feel slighted in any way, rather than confronting you about the perceived injustice, and this can be dangerous to work efficiency.*
>
> (British expatriate, 50–54 years old, Financial Services)

Lead by Example Another suggestion made by the expatriates was to listen more, be coherent with one's words and lead by example. Some of them had rolled up their sleeves and showed their Thai staff the way by doing it themselves. They said that leading by example 'made the Thais want to do things better than you' and is an effective approach to earn the Thai staff's respect as they see you as a model from which to learn. A senior American expatriate stated:

> *Leading is doing here. A leader has to become more of a player/coach [instead of] just a coach.*
> (American expatriate, 55–59 years old, Automotive, Power Equipment & Food)

Leading by example was seen by some expatriates as the most effective approach to leading Thai employees, particularly when they wanted to change things. Thai employees are more willing to follow the lead when they have a role model and when they are shown how things are done. On the other hand, a leader who talks the talk but does not walk the walk can hardly make any changes as the Thai staff will continue doing what they have always done.

GIVE CLEAR, SIMPLE INSTRUCTIONS, CHECK UNDERSTANDING, AND MONITOR PROGRESS

Another main suggestion given by the expatriates was to provide staff with clear task instructions, checking whether they had understood the task and process, and monitoring the progress. They said that Thai employees were efficient when they performed a task which was 'standardized in a clear sequence, with no loopholes' and when they were given one task at a time. Thus, they suggested making tasks as simple as possible, giving employees complete and clear instructions and explaining the intended outcomes. An American expatriate stated,

I have been here for almost 20 years now and it is a continuous battle to get things done. The adjustment that needs to be made is to make everything as simple as possible and to not make them do or think too much at the same time. There is no such thing as multi-tasking here.
(American expatriate, 45–49 years old, Consulting)

The root cause behind the lack of ability to deal with multiple or complicated tasks was thought to be down to the Thai education system not being designed to encourage critical thinking.

To accommodate the Thai employees' need for simple, linear tasks, some expatriates said that they had to identify issues and problems early. An expatriate said that he had to design work sequences, with forms and handbooks, for every task; and others said that they had to show examples of how to do tasks.

Ensuring that instructions, processes, expectations and responsibilities are well-understood by the staff is also important in order to avoid any misunderstandings caused by language barriers and by the Thai employees' tendency to say 'yes' rather than ask a question. In addition, it is suggested to frequently follow up on the work progress and ensure that instructions are being carried out. An expatriate from Italy suggested the following:

> *The Thai people require much more detailed instructions and deadlines; things cannot be said and expected to be done without a well-structured plan. Never, ever assume. Be as clear as possible, you can never be TOO clear. Confirm verbally or in written form (written is always better) that you have a mutual understanding. When starting in a new job, always schedule shorter checkpoints to avoid misunderstanding and steep deviations to your original plan. Communicate as often as possible, not just about the plan, but sometimes just [leave] your desk and walk [among] your staff just to see how they're doing or if they need help with anything.*
> (Italian expatriate, 35–39 years old, IT/e-commerce)

Many expatriates indicated that, although more time is needed for completing tasks in Thailand, Thai employees eventually get there. They suggested that the only way forward was to allow extra time and process the procedures step by step, point by point which could be done by explaining the strategy, the decisions, the processes, the expected outcomes to monitor work progress. Several managers said that they had to use more 'micro-management', even with senior Thai staff. Two expatriates said,

> *[...] you have to check almost everything in detail as tasks can get stuck or go wrong and you will never know about it.*
> (French expatriate, 55–59 years old, Decoration)

> *[...] leadership style needs to be different. Much less confrontational, more holding hands and much more repeating of the message. If you don't do these things, things won't get done and people [will] just continue the way they always [had].*
> (Dutch expatriate, 45–49 years old, Financial outsourcing services)

AVOID THAI STAFF LOSING FACE

As illustrated in chapter 6, some expatriates perceived the issue of 'face' as one of the major challenges in leading Thai employees. Many of them said that it is important to ensure that Thai staff do not lose face in front of others and suggested the following points:

- Understand the concept of 'face'.

- Avoid any situations that might lead to staff losing face.

- Never embarrass Thai employees, to avoid causing them to lose face.

- Do not publicly confront or challenge Thai staff when something goes wrong, to avoid them losing face in front of others.

- Only give negative feedback in private on a one-on-one basis.

- Congratulate in public and reprimand behind closed doors.

- Thai employees may resign if they lose face, so give them an 'out' when things go wrong.

- Find alternatives or different methods to discipline employees when necessary.

- If there are difficulties with employees, address the issues in private and with a softer approach and less directly than North American or Europeans typically would.

BUILD TRUSTING RELATIONSHIPS

A number of expatriates expressed that gaining the trust of Thai staff is key to leading them successfully. The following quotes illustrate the experiences of some of the expatriates:

> *I have been working in Asia for the past 20 years – in Japan, Singapore, India and Thailand – as an expat. I find that you need to gain the trust of your employees to be successful.*
> (American expatriate, 55–59 years old, Semiconductor Manufacturing)

> *I found that getting into people's hearts and gaining their trust*

has brought about an amazing level of support and loyalty. Simple, regular events such as eating together – a great basic trait in food-focused Thailand – helps alleviate stress and promote team bonding.

(Australian expatriate, 45–49 years old, Hospitality)

I have been working in South East Asia for 20 years for a large variety of businesses in the service industry. The key to success is always the same: building positive relationships of trust and mutual respect from day one onward with the management team and the whole workforce, including third party businesses. It is the best way to be successful and efficient and to work in a positive environment.

(Nationality unknown, 45–49 years old, Hospitality)

Sharing experiences and food and developing an emotional connection were mentioned to be good ways of building trust and relationships. Building trust, however, is not an easy task. Some expatriates said that it took much longer to build trust in Thailand than in other Asian countries and that it was an ongoing process. An American expatriate said,

One of the main challenges is building enough trust to be able to communicate directly and receive a direct communication in return. This is an ongoing and never quite complete process. Consistent reassurances are required to create a consequence-free communication environment that everyone believes in.

(American expatriate, 35–39 years old, Legal Services)

Building trust was considered a long process because Thais have a very tight circle of family and friends and they are generally diffident and suspicious of people outside of these two inner circles. Nevertheless, once a trusting relationship is established, the expatriates said, many good things followed. For example, the team responded well to changes; they frankly expressed their ideas and opinions; and they showed willingness to do their jobs.

OVERCOME LANGUAGE BARRIERS

As described in chapter 8, communication and language barriers are regarded as a major challenge in leading Thai employees. As a matter of fact, getting messages across is challenging for both the expatriates and locals as, in most situations, the expatriate managers cannot communicate in Thai; on the other hand, the locals, although they do have some ability to communicate in English, do not have the depth of vocabulary needed for a detailed understanding.

81

Several expatriates suggested that learning to speak some basic Thai will bring the following benefits:

- helping to reduce the number of mistakes caused by misunderstanding
- helping to better understand Thai culture
- gaining the appreciation of the employees
- helping integration with Thai staff
- helping to build good working relationships with Thai staff

SPEND MORE TIME ON COACHING AND DEVELOPMENT

Investing more time on employee development was another suggestion made by the expatriates. It is necessary because the expatriates feel that their Thai staff are not provided with sufficient developmental activities to help them grow personally and professionally. The approaches they adopted for employee development mainly included training, coaching and mentoring. For training, activities such as on-the-job training, hands-on activities and role-play were seen to be more effective than classroom teaching. For coaching and mentoring, personal and one-to-one coaching were seen as key.

A variety of contents was included in developmental activities. For example, the expatriates trained their staff in how to perform well in their roles, in the skill sets needed in an international firm (e.g. being able to make a confident presentation and work autonomously) and in how to be critical and how to continuously challenge themselves. They motivated their staff; they shared and explained the intended team outcomes; and they provided honest feedback.

The key areas upon which the expatriates focused were developing their staff's critical thinking and problem solving skills and building their confidence to express their opinions and dissent. These were regarded as areas of weakness, as described in chapter 6. Two expatriates said,

> We spend a lot of time encouraging our staff to participate and ask questions in team meetings.
> (Australian expatriate, 35–39 years old, Food Manufacturing)

> I have been constantly changing the way of working within the three companies I have worked with in Thailand [...] the main thing I have been changing is the need to think outside of the box, to be proactive and improve efficiency.
> (British expatriate, 40–44 years old, Financial Services)

Many expatriates were positive about the potential of their staff and the developmental efforts made. They tried to help their staff to think like managers and to grow into the professionals they knew they could be. Some expatriates said that they found most of their employees to be quick learners once they were shown the way. Two expatriates said,

> You can always change Thai people by providing more training all the time. It's not easy to change them from one day to the other; however, when proper training is provided and explained, then change starts to take place.
> (Armenian expatriate, 40–44 years old, Manufacturing)

> It does take longer for my Thai staff to develop the confidence that their opinions and ideas matter and, on many occasions, are better than mine or those of other managers. But, once they gain that confidence, the team works like any I have been part of or managed elsewhere.
> (British expatriate, 45–49 years old, Automotive, Fast Food Retail, and other sectors)

Other expatriates watched most of their staff progress up the career ladder through their developmental efforts, although they also observed that a small number of staff were not motivated. Two expatriates stated,

> Through continuous coaching, you try to bring your employees to the next level, and, with most people, it works, but, with others, it doesn't.
> (Belgian expatriates, 45–49 years old, Plastic Packaging)

> I also try to train them to be critical of every step of a process and continuously challenge themselves. Some staff pick up on it and have been able to grow substantially in their careers. From my Thai staff at the HOD level, seven have become Resident Managers and two General Managers. I see potential in them, brains that can be trained to think. I then spend more time on them to develop. Others are just not interested and want the easy Thai way. No hassle and take it easy.
> (Dutch expatriates, 45–49 years old, Hospitality)

Some expatriates used a roadmap for skill development and provided feedback and recognition through coaching. A British expatriate shared his approach:

A roadmap seems to serve employees well for keeping them motivated and building confidence in their work performance [...] I try to coach regularly and have others coach their direct [employees], modelling behaviours and skills and giving regular feedback and recognition [...] I'm a big believer in genuine recognition and feedback.
(British expatriate, 55–59 years old, Corporate Training)

In addition to the developmental activities delivered locally, an expatriate mentioned that his company provided a corporate leadership development training programme for Thai staff with high potential, which rotated them among different operational sites within Asia and went beyond functional skill training.

ENCOURAGE STAFF MEMBERS TO TAKE INITIATIVES AND RESPONSIBILITIES

As described earlier, one of the challenges faced by the leaders in leading Thai employees was related to the staff's lack of initiative. Many expatriates stated that, in most cases, Thai employees would report issues but would not proactively come up with potential solutions as they expected the most senior person to do so; so staff brought problems, not solutions.

To encourage staff to take initiatives and responsibilities, most of the expatriates said they used *empowerment and delegation*. Different expatriates adopted different approaches when exercising these. Below, I summarise the main approaches.

Making Thai staff feel secure in making decisions   Some expatriates said that the fear of making wrong decisions and dealing with the resulting consequences or criticisms was a key reason for Thai employees not liking to take initiatives and make decisions. To tackle this, some expatriates said that they had made it very clear to their staff that if something went wrong, the responsibility still resided with senior management. This made staff feel secure in making decisions and stopped them from resigning if they made a mistake.

Supporting empowerment through training and coaching   To make empowerment and delegation effective, the expatiates provided support for their staff's work. Some of them gave their staff enough information to help them try and solve a problem or perform a task using their own initiatives. Some encouraged their Thai staff to take risks and initiatives, allowing them to make mistakes and urging them to learn from these instead of making them feel that they had not succeeded. Others trained and taught their staff ways to put forward their views, take initiatives, make decisions and be critical. What the expatriates aimed at doing was to give their staff the ability and confidence to volunteer their opinions, take efficient initiatives, and assume more responsibilities.

Encouraging employees to put forward their ideas in relaxed environments   Many expatriates said that they encouraged their Thai staff to put forward their own ideas instead of relying on senior people. Some of them tried to encourage initiatives and sharing of ideas by making it clear that all ideas are good. They did so in relaxed environments, like coffee bars or over lunch, rather than in meeting rooms. They rewarded those who brought new perspectives and those who challenged senior people for the benefit of the business. Others encouraged staff to ask questions and challenge the viewpoints of senior management in order to break down the hierarchical system.

Establishing a standardised reporting practice to encourage accountability   Some expatriates established a standardised reporting process with the aim of helping staff learn to take responsibility and to solve problems. Two expatriates described how they used standardised approaches to promote the taking of initiatives and responsibilities:

> In typical circumstances, an issue would arrive fully articulated, but with no suggestions for resolution and no recommendation about [which] resolution option would be the most effective. Over a period of several months, I established a standard practice for any person who visited my office with an issue. I developed a work ethos [by which] individuals or teams with issues would arrive at my office fully prepared to immerse me in the issue, present the options and then argue the case for the option they believed was the best resolution. This became a very time-efficient process, with the added benefit of giving the teams a genuine sense of empowerment.
> (Indian expatriate, 55–59 years old, Information Technology and Consulting)

> I try to [encourage] foremen and sub-contractors to first [evaluate] whether I would accept their standard of work before presenting it to me as complete. Always review when something is wrong or is right with your staff and then ensure

they either correct it or are praised for their good work. This way, you can get them to take ownership or responsibility of the work they are in charge of.
(British expatriate, 45–49 years old, Engineering)

Developing a sense of responsibility through projects Some expatriates tried to develop their staff's sense of responsibility and proactivity by giving them projects in areas that interested them. In these projects, different staff members were given different responsibilities.

Delegating less responsibility to individuals at a time Some expatriates used what they called a 'micro leaders' approach. In this approach, they organised smaller teams with more leaders, each having less responsibility, rather than large teams with fewer leaders with all the responsibility.

Raising staff confidence Compared to western employees, some expatriates observed that most Thai ones lack confidence or belief in their own ability. They therefore worked on raising their staff's self-confidence and helping them see that they were a valuable asset to the company and that the company really needed, and valued, their input and ideas.

Were all the efforts described above and aimed at encouraging staff to take initiatives and responsibilities worth making? Some expatriates said that their efforts paid off and that their staff had become willing to make decisions and take on responsibilities. An Australian expatriate said,

> *In my experience, the staff were pleased to make decisions and, over time, took on responsibility willingly. They gladly initiated projects necessary for running the business.*
(Australian expatriate, 50–54 years old, Marketing)

BUILD A WORKING ENVIRONMENT CONDUCIVE TO OPEN COMMUNICATION

Another suggestion made by the expatriates was creating an open, friendly working environment that allows employees to communicate openly. Many of the expatriates said that they spent more time on communication in Thailand than in other locations. They said that they found time to communicate with their staff wherever possible in order to hear ideas and viewpoints from all levels, not just from those in senior positions. Some did so through one-to-one meetings/discussions that often took place on a weekly or bi-monthly basis and involved a third person with good English skills.

Many of them pointed out that, in Thailand, many things could only be done through constant two-way communication. Taking as an example making changes to existing work practices, several expatriates said that, in Thailand, making changes should be approached carefully and required quite a bit of work. They said that, on the one hand, they needed to explain, as much as possible, the reasons for a change, the expected outcomes and benefits, why standing still cannot be an option, and why change was important to the organization and their clients. On the other hand, they had to understand the employees' concerns, ask for their opinions, and come to an agreement with the staff.

In addition to enhancing communication between their employees and themselves, some expatriates made an effort to enhance communication between business units. A British expatriate stated:

> I ensure that we have regular meetings and share more what is going on across the business. I want to connect more parts of the business and drive stronger communication. In most cases, in Thailand, the business units rarely speak to each other – so a chance to drive great teamwork and synergy is important when leading.
>
> (British expatriate, 40–44 years old, Healthcare)

Many expatriates indicated that they had endeavoured to create a culture of open communication so that their employees would feel comfortable and confident to come forward with their own views and discuss issues openly. This is necessary as most Thai employees tend not to express their opinions and often perceive negative feedback as a personal criticism.

BUILD A FUN AND RELAXED WORKING ENVIRONMENT

Several expatriates suggested that building a fun and relaxed working environment is important for effectively leading Thai employees. These expatriates were not only from those industry sectors usually linked with 'fun', such as hospitality, IT and marketing, but also from some normally pictured as having a more serious working atmosphere, such as legal services, healthcare, government, real estate and manufacturing.

They said that Thai staff are comfortable with 'social' approaches and like to have fun in the workplace, and that leaders would achieve more if they approached things "in a light manner and have fun with it" as Thai staff have a 'sanuk' (สนุก, which means to have fun, to enjoy oneself and to achieve satisfaction and pleasure from whatever you do) attitude and they want to bring fun aspects to work and life. A British expatriate said,

> [...] working under stress seems to worry Thais more, it's important to keep things fun and light hearted, not too serious.
> (British expatriate, 40–44 years old, Market Research)

Two more expatriates expressed the same view and emphasized the importance of having fun elements in the workplace:

> Another important point is that you need to provide [them with] fun at work. Thais do not consider life as a boring experience, they really expect to have fun even at the office. So it's very important to bring them some fun and activities. However, you need to keep your distance with your employees [...] you represent the power, so you need to wear the attributes of power and show them (proper dress code, strong decision making skills, ability of clearly explaining your objectives, paying for some treats, food, parties, driving a beautiful car...)
> (French expatriate, 40–44 years old, IT Development)

> Leading Thai people is very different from leading staff from other countries [...] The key to success is sanuk or, in other words, creating a trustful and balanced work environment that is challenging but leaves room for fun and laughter. When this gets out of balance, the staff is quick to resign; hence, managing the balance between sanuk and hard business goals is the key challenge as a leader [...] I have adjusted in terms of listening more, being less formal and strict as I have to manage business and the sanuk factor. I learned the hard way that following the western approach [resulted in] being suddenly confronted with resignations as there was too much pressure.
> (Dutch expatriate, 45–49 years old, Manufacturing)

To create a fun atmosphere, a German expatriate sponsored punctuality awards, in a gamely fashion, to encourage staff to meet deadlines and come to meetings and events on time. A British expatriate said that Thais love working in groups and that leaders will be more effective if they can incorporate 'fun' and 'team' concepts into the workplace.

Chapter Nine Executive Summary
Insights and Suggestions for Leading Thai Employees
Effectively

- This chapter presents the main suggestions made by the expatriate business leaders for leading Thai employees effectively. Their suggestions are:

  o **Learn, be mindful of, respect, and accept social and cultural expectations and differences:** many of the expatriate leaders said that Western methods rarely worked without modification in Thailand, and suggested that it was crucial to understand and respect the cultural and societal norms and expectations and learn to work within their boundaries. In particular, they emphasised the importance of understanding the concepts of 'face' and *Kreng Jai* , the conflict avoidance mentality and soft approach of Thai employees, and their respect for seniors and elders.

  o **Adjust your own emotions and behaviours:** the expatriates stated that it had been important for them to adjust their own emotions and behaviours in order to be accepted by Thai employees. They suggested that other expatriates: a) adopt an indirect approach in order to avoid causing offence to Thai employees and trigger emotional reactions in them; b) be patient, learn to slow down and approach issues over time; c) stay calm in all situations and at all times and not loose their temper in front of their Thai employees; d) adopt a soft, harmonious and relationship-based approach; and e) listen more, stand by their word and lead by example.

  o **Give clear, simple instructions, check understanding, and monitor progress:** the expatriates said that Thai employees were efficient when performing simple, linear, and standardized tasks. Thus, they suggested making tasks as simple as possible, giving employees complete and clear instructions and explaining the intended outcomes. They also highlighted the need to check whether instructions, processes, expectations, and responsibilities were well-understood by the staff and frequently follow up on the work progress.

  o **Avoid Thai staff losing face:** many of the expatriates observed that their Thai employees saw 'face' as something that was extremely important to be upheld;

thus, they suggested to avoid any situations that might lead to staff losing face. For example, avoiding negative feedback or confronting Thai staff in front of others in the event of things going wrong.

- **Build trusting relationships:** a number of expatriates stated that gaining the trust of their Thai staff had been key to leading them successfully. The expatriates said that, although gaining the trust of their Thai employees had been a long and on-going process, once a trusting relationship had been established, many good things followed. For example, their teams had responded well to changes, had expressed their ideas and opinions frankly, and had showed willingness to do their jobs.

- **Overcome language barriers:** several expatriates suggested that learning to speak some basic Thai would help better understand Thai culture, gain the appreciation of the employees, integrate and build good working relationships with Thai staff, and reduce the number of mistakes caused by misunderstandings.

- **Spend more time on coaching and development:** many of the expatriates suggested to invest more time on coaching and development to help employees grow both personally and professionally. They were positive about the potential of their staff and the developmental efforts made.

- **Encourage staff members to take initiatives and responsibilities:** several approaches had been used to encourage Thai staff members to take initiatives and responsibilities, these included making them feel secure in making decisions, supporting their empowerment through training and coaching, encouraging them to put forward their ideas in relaxed environments, establishing standardised reporting practices to encourage accountability, developing a sense of responsibility through projects, raising confidence, and delegating less responsibility to individuals at a time.

- **Build a working environment conducive to open communication:** many of the expatriates said that they had spent more time on communication in Thailand than in other locations and that they had endeavoured to create a culture of open communication so that their employees would feel comfortable and confident to come forward with their own views and discuss issues openly.

- ○ **Build a fun and relaxed working environment:** several expatriates said that their Thai employees were comfortable with 'social' approaches and liked to have fun in the workplace; they thus suggested that leaders would achieve more if they approached things in a light manner and built a fun and relaxed working environment.

CHAPTER 10. CONCLUSION

The rapid growth of the international business market makes it important for business leaders to understand how to effectively influence and manage employees with different cultural values, expectations, attitudes, and behaviours. My research has sought to explore the adjustment behaviours of expatriate senior business leaders working in the foreign cultural setting of Thailand. The results of the research show that most expatriate business leaders simultaneously adjusted their leadership approaches and tried to change their Thai employees, thus demonstrating the adoption of the *exploration* mode of adjustment. They did so because, on the one hand, they thought that it was necessary to align their leadership approaches with their followers' characteristics and, on the other hand, they perceived that it was also necessary to change such characteristics. Therefore, they simultaneously adjusted their leadership approaches (e.g., by adopting less direct and more diplomatic ones) and tried to change their Thai staff members (e.g., by encouraging them to be more expressive) in order to meet the local conditions and to match their personal requirements.

In this book, I showed that the leaders faced a number of challenges and reported how they tried to meet them. The challenges mentioned in the book and the ability of the companies to achieve their business goals will be determined by the role, strength, quality, and adaptability of the leadership demonstrated by their senior managers, whose key task is to deliver results by leading people.

The implications that can be derived from my research are that effectively influencing and managing employees from different cultural contexts requires gaining a good understanding of their work attitudes and behaviours and adjusting and conforming to local societal norms. Deviation from the latter may result in employee resistance, diminished respect toward managers, high employee turnover, and decreased leader effectiveness. Leadership adjustment, therefore, is central to the effective management of human resources in cross-cultural contexts.

My research underlines the need for more empirical research on cross-cultural leadership adjustment in order to provide insights for situational leadership theories. The two leadership theories discussed in chapter two—SLT and CLTs—both advocate that, to be effective, leadership approaches should be adjusted to address the characteristics of followers. In practice, however, we know very little about the extent to which expatriate business leaders adjust their leadership approaches to cater to the characteristics of their host country employees. More research in this area is needed in order to help us understand the dynamics of leadership behaviour in cross-cultural contexts.

I hope this book will help expatriate managers to understand the unique values, and attitudes of Thai employees and to anticipate and respond effectively to local workplace behaviours and practices. I also hope this book will inspire more researchers to conduct cross-cultural leadership research to provide us with more insights into this important area of international management.

References

Adsit, D. J., London, M., Crom, S., & Jones, D. (1997). Cross-cultural differences in upward ratings in a multinational company. *International Journal of Human Resource Management, 8*, 385-401.

Austrade. (2016). Doing business, Export markets – Thailand. [Online] Australian Trade Commission. Available from: http://www.austrade.gov.au/Australian/Export/Export-markets/Countries/Thailand/Doing-business [Accessed 4th April 2016].

Bass, B. M., & Stogdill, R. M. (1990). *Handbook of Leadership: Theory, Research and Managerial Applications*. New York: Free Press.

Black, J. S. (1988). Work role transitions: a study of American expatriate mangers in Japan. *Journal of International Business Studies, 19*, 277-294.

Black, J. S., Mendenhall, M., & Oddou, G. (1991). Toward a comprehensive model of international adjustment: an integration of multiple theoretical perspectives. *Academy of Management Review, 16*, 291-317.

Black, J. S., & Stephens, G. K. (1989). The Influence of the Spouse on American Expatriate Adjustment and Intent to Stay in Pacific Rim Overseas Assignments. *Journal of Management, 15*, 529.

BoI. (2016a). Doing Buiness/Thailand/Demographic. [Online] The Board of Investment of Thailand. Available from: http://www.boi.go.th/index.php?page=demographic&language=en [Accessed 25th July 2016].

BoI. (2016b). Economic Overview/Thailand's Economic Outlook 2016. [Online] The Board of Investment of Thailand. Available from: http://www.boi.go.th/index.php?page=economic_overview [Accessed 27th July 2016].

BoI. (2016c). Thailand's Rankings. [Online] The Board of Investment of Thailand. Available from: http://www.boi.go.th/index.php?page=thailand_rankings [Accessed 1st August 2016].

Brodbeck, F. C., Frese, M., Akerblom, S., Audia, G., Bakacsi, G., Bendova, H., Bodega, D., Bodur, M., Booth, S., Brenk, K., Castel, P., Hartog, D. D., Donnelly-Cox, G., Gratchev, M. V., Holmberg, I., Jarmuz, S., Jesuino, J. C., Jorbenadse, R., Kabasakal, H. E., & Keating, M. (2000). Cultural variation of leadership prototypes across 22 European countries. *Journal of Occupational & Organizational Psychology, 73*, 1-29.

Brodbeck, F. C., Frese, M., & Javidan, M. (2002). Leadership made in Germany: Low on compassion, high on performance. *Academy of Management Executive, 16*, 16-29.

Chompookum, D., & Brooklyn Derr, C. (2004). The effects of internal career orientations on organizational citizenship behavior in Thailand. *Career Development International, 9*, 406-423.

CIA. (2016). The world Factbook: East & Suthease Asia: Thailand. [Online] Central Intelligence Agency. Available from: https://www.cia.gov/library/publications/the-world-factbook/geos/th.html [Accessed 1st August 2016].

Den Hartog, D. N., House, R. J., Hanges, P. J., Ruiz-Quintanilla, S. A., & Dorfman, P. W. (1999). Culture specific and cross-culturally generalizable implicit leadership theories: are attributes of charismatic/transformational leadership universally endorsed? *Leadership Quarterly, 10*, 219.

Dickson, M. W., Den Hartog, D. N., & Mitchelson, J. K. (2003). Research on leadership in a cross-cultural context: Making progress, and raising new questions. *The Leadership Quarterly, 14*, 729-768.

Dorfman, P. W., Hanges, P. J., & Brodbeck, F. C. (2004). Leadership and Culture Variation: The Identification of Culturally Endorsed Leadership Profiles. In R. J. House, P. J. Hanges, M. Javidan, P. W. Dorfman & V. Gupta (Eds.), *Leadership, Culture, and Organizations: The GLOBE Study of 62 Societies* (pp. 669–719). Thousand Oaks, CA: Sage.

Dorfman, P. W., Howell, J. P., Hibino, S., Lee, J. K., Tate, U., & Bautista, A. (1997). Leadership in Western and Asian countries: Commonalities and differences in effective leadership processes across cultures. *The Leadership Quarterly, 8*, 233-274.

Ducanes, G., & Abella, M. (2013). *Labour Shortages, Foreign Migrant Recruitment and the Portability of Qualifications in East and South-East Asia*: ILO.

ExpatArrivals. (2016). Doing Business in Thailand. [Online] Expat Arrivals. Available from: http://www.expatarrivals.com/thailand/doing-business-in-thailand [Accessed 28th April 2016].

Fairchild, C. (2014). Women CEOs in the Fortune 1000: By the numbers. In *FORTUNE Magazine* 8 July. Available from: <http://fortune.com/2014/07/08/women-ceos-fortune-500-1000/>. [15 April 2015].

Festing, M., & Maletzky, M. (2011). Cross-cultural leadership adjustment — A multilevel framework based on the theory of structuration. *Human Resource Management Review, 21*, 186-200.

Fiedler, F. E. (1967). A Theory of Leadership Effectiveness. In. New York: McGraw-Hill.

FocusEconomics. (2015). Thai government introduces new stimulus package to revitalize the underperforming economy. [Online] Focus Economics, 22nd September. Available from: http://www.focus-economics.com/countries/thailand/news/politics/thai-government-introduces-new-stimulus-package-to-revitalize-the [Accessed 27th March 2016].

Goffman, E. (1955). On facewor. *Psychiatry*, 213–231.

Graeff, C. L. (1983). The situational leadership theory: a critical view. *Academy of Management Review, 8*, 285-291.

Hemphill, J. K. (1949). *Situational Factors in Leadership*. Columbus, Ohio: State University.

Hersey, P., & Blanchard, K. (1972). *Management of Organizational Behavior (2nd ed.)*. Englewood Cliffs: NJ: Prentice-Hall.

Hersey, P., & Blanchard, K. (1982). Management of organizational behavior: Utilizing human resources (4th ed.). In. Englewood Cliffs: NJ: Prentice-Hall.

Ho, D. Y.-f. (1976). On the concept of face. *American journal of sociology*, 867-884.

Hollander, E. P., & Offermann, L. R. (1990). Power and leadership in organizations: relationships in transition. *American Psychologist, 45*, 179-189.

Holmes, H., Tangtongtavy, S., & Tomizawa, R. (1995). *Working with the Thais: A guide to managing in Thailand*: White Lotus.

House, R. (1971). A Path Goal Theory of Leader Effectiveness. *Administrative Science Quarterly, 16*, 321-339.

House, R., & Aditya, R. N. (1997). The social scientific study of leadership: quo vadis? *Journal of Management, 23*, 409-473.

House, R., Javidan, M., Hanges, P., & Dorfman, P. (2002). Understanding cultures and implicit leadership theories across the globe: an introduction to project GLOBE. *Journal of World Business, 37*, 3-11.

House, R. J., Hanges, P. J., Javidan, M., Dorfman, P., & Gupta, V. (2004). Culture, leadership, and organizations: The GLOBE study of 62 societies. In. Thousand Oaks, CA: Sage Publications.

House, R. J., Hanges, P. J., Javidan, M., Dorfman, P. W., & Gupta, V. (2004). *Culture, leadership, and organizations: The GLOBE study of 62 societies*: Sage publications.

Hu, H. C. (1944). The Chinese concepts of "face". *American Anthropologist, 46*, 45-64.

Javidan, M., & Carl, D. E. (2005). Leadership across cultures: a study of Canadian and Taiwanese executives. *Management International Review (MIR), 45*, 23-44.

Javidan, M., Dorfman, P. W., De Luque, M. S., & House, R. (2006). In the eye of the beholder: cross cultural lessons in leadership from project GLOBE. *Academy of Management Perspectives, 20*, 67-90.

Jingjit, R., & Fotaki, M. (2011). Confucian ethics and the limited impact of the new public management reform in Thailand. *Journal of Business Ethics, 104*, 61-73.

Keyes, C. F. (1989). Buddhist politics and their revolutionary origins in Thailand. *International Political Science Review, 10*, 121-142.

Kim, J. Y., & Nam, S. H. (1998). The concept and dynamics of face: Implications for organizational behavior in Asia. *Organization Science, 9*, 522-534.

Komin, S. (1990). Culture and work-related values in Thai organizations. *International Journal of Psychology, 25*, 681-704.

Lee, C., & Green, R. T. (1991). Cross-cultural examination of the Fishbein behavioral intentions model. *Journal of International Business Studies, 22*, 289-305.

Lee, K., Scandura, T. A., & Sharif, M. M. (2014). Cultures have consequences: A configural approach to leadership across two cultures. *The Leadership Quarterly, 25*, 692-710.

Leung, S. L., & Bozionelos, N. (2004). Five-factor model traits and the prototypical image of the effective leader in the Confucian culture. *Employee Relations, 26*, 62-71.

LindedIn. (2014). About LinkedIn. [Online] LinkedIn. Available from http://press.linkedin.com/about [Accessed 24th October 2014].

Lord, R. G., Binning, J. F., Rush, M. C., & Thomas, J. C. (1978). The Effect of Performance Cues and Leader Behavior on Questionnaire Ratings of Leadership Behavior. *Organizational Behavior & Human Performance, 21*, 27-39.

Lord, R. G., De Vader, C., & Alliger, G. M. (1986). A meta-analysis of the relation between personality traits and leadership perceptions: an application of validity generalization procedures. *Journal of Applied Psychology, 71*, 402-410.

Lord, R. G., Foti, R. J., & De Vader, C. L. (1984). A Test of Leadership Categorization Theory: Internal Structure, Information Processing, and Leadership Perceptions. *Organizational Behavior & Human Performance, 34*, 343-378.

Lord, R. G., & Maher, K. J. (1991). Leadership and information processing: Linking perceptions and performance. In. Cambridge: MA: Unwin Hyman.

Morris, N. (2013). Number of female executives at FTSE 100 companies is falling despite efforts to boost women in industry. In *The Independent*. 19 June. Available from: <http://www.independent.co.uk/news/uk/politics/number-of-female-executives-at-ftse-100-companies-is-falling-despite-efforts-to-boost-women-in-industry-8665183.html>. [15 April 2015].

Morrison, A. M., & Von Glinow, M.-A. (1990). Women and minorities in management. *American Psychologist, 45*, 200-208.

Mullins, J. (1999). Management and Organizational Behavior. In: Prentice Hall International.

Nahavandi, A. (2006). *The art and science of leadership.* Upper Saddle River, NJ: Prentice Hall.

Nicholson, N. (1984). A theory of work role transitions. *Administrative Science Quarterly, 29*, 172-191.

Nlambassade. (2016). Business Etiquette in Thailand. [Online] Embassy of the Kingdom of the Netherlands in Bangkok Thailand. Available from: http://thailand.nlambassade.org/landeninformatie/handel-en-investeren/zakendoen-in-thailand/zakelijke-gedragsregels-copy.html [Accessed 4th April 2016].

Northouse, P. G. (2006). Leadership: Theory and practice (4th ed.). In. Thousand Oaks: Sage.

Northouse, P. G. (2007). Leadership: Theory and practice. In. Thousand Oaks: CA: Sage Publications.

NSO. (2016). Industrial Census, year 2012. [Online] National Statistical Office of Thailand. Available from: http://web.nso.go.th/en/survey/construction/industrial_12.htm [Accessed 28th March 2016].

NSO. (2016a). Summary of the labor force survey in Thailand : December 2015. [Online] National Statistical Office, Thailand. Available from: http://web.nso.go.th/en/survey/data_survey/050259_summary_December 58.pdf [Accessed 25th July 2016].

NSO. (2016b). Key indicators of the population and housing 1980 – 2010. [Online] National Statistical Office, Thailand. Available from: http://popcensus.nso.go.th/quick_stat1.php?rg=1 [Accessed 25th July 2016].

Peltokorpi, V., & Froese, F. J. (2012). The impact of expatriate personality traits on cross-cultural adjustment: A study with expatriates in Japan. *International Business Review, 21*, 734-746.

Pornpitakpan, C. (2000). Trade in Thailand: A three-way cultural comparison. *Business Horizons, 43*, 61-70.

Ravasi, C., Salamin, X., & Davoine, E. (2015). Cross-cultural adjustment of skilled migrants in a multicultural and multilingual environment: an explorative study of foreign employees and their spouses in the Swiss context. *The International Journal of Human Resource Management, 26*, 1335-1359.

Reddin, W. J. (1967). The 3-D Management Style Theory. *Training & Development Journal, 21*, 8.

Rotter, J. B. (1966). Generalized expectancies for internal versus external control of reinforcement. *Psychological monographs: General and applied, 80*, 1.

Rotter, J. B. (1975). Some problems and misconceptions related to the construct of internal versus external control of reinforcement. *Journal of consulting and clinical psychology, 43*, 56.

Shaffer, M. A., Harrison, D. A., & Gilley, K. M. (1999). Dimensions, Determinants, and Differences in the Expatriate Adjustment Process. *Journal of International Business Studies, 30*, 557-581.

Siengthai, S., & Vadhanasindhu, P. (1991). "Management in the Buddhist society", in Putti, J. (Eds.). In *Management: Asian Context*: McGraw-Hill Book Co.

Siengthi, S., & Bechter, C. (2004). HRM in Thailand. In Budhwar, P. (Ed.). In *Managing Human Resource in Asia-Pacific* (pp. 141-172). London: Routledge.

Simintiras, A. C., & Thomas, A. H. (1998). Cross-cultural sales negotiations: A literature review and research propositions. *International Marketing Review, 15*, 10-28.

Simonton, D. K. (1994). Greatness: Who Makes History and Why. In. New York: The Guilford Press.

Sriussadaporn, R. (2006). Managing international business communication problems at work: a pilot study in foreign companies in Thailand. *Cross Cultural Management: An International Journal, 13*, 330-344.

Stogdill, R. M. (1950). Leadership, membership and organization. *Psychological Bulletin, 47*, 1-14.

Thatcher, B. (2001). Issues of validity in intercultural professional communication research. *Journal of Business and Technical Communication, 15*, 458-489.

Thompson, G., & Vecchio, R. P. (2009). Situational leadership theory: A test of three versions. *Leadership Quarterly, 20*, 837-848.

Thorelli, H. B., & Sentell, G. D. (1982). *Consumer emancipation and economic development: The case of Thailand.* Greenwich: CT: JAI Press.

UKTI. (2016). Thailand Business Guide. [Online] UK Trade and Investment. Available from: www.ukabc.org.uk/?attachment_id=123 [Accessed 27th March 2016].

UNCTAD. (2016). World Investment Prospect Survey 2014 –2016. [Online] United Nations Conference on Trade and Development. Available from: http://unctad.org/en/PublicationsLibrary/webdiaeia2015d4_en.pdf [Accessed 1st August 2016].

Vecchio, R. P. (1987). Situational leadership theory: An examination of a prescriptive theory. *Journal of Applied Psychology, 72*, 444-451.

Vroom, V. H., & Yetton, P. W. (1974). Leadership and decision-making. In. Pittsburgh: University of Pittsburgh Press.

Warner, M. (2003). *Culture and Management in Asia.* London: Routledge.

WorldBank. (2016a). Ease of doing business index. [Online] World Bank. Available from: http://data.worldbank.org/indicator/IC.BUS.EASE.XQ [Accessed 9th October 2016].

WorldBank. (2016b). Unemployment Data. [Online] World Bank. Available from: http://data.worldbank.org/indicator/SL.UEM.TOTL.ZS [Accessed 27th April 2016].

Yang, M. C. (1945). *A Chinese Village: Taitou, Shatung Province, .* New York: Columbia University Press.

Yukl, G. (1998). Leadership in organizations. In. Englewood Cliffs, NJ: Prentice-Hall.

Yukl, G. (2006). Leadership in organizations. In. Upper Saddle River: NJ: Prentice-Hall.

Zimmermann, A., & Sparrow, P. (2007). Mutual adjustment processes in international teams. *International Studies of Management & Organization, 37*, 65-88.

Appendix. Online survey questions

1. Is leading Thai subordinates different from leading subordinates in your home country? What are the similarities and differences? What are the challenges?

2. Do you have to adjust your leadership approach working in Thailand at all? If so, what do you have to adjust? What leads to the need for adjustment?
   How do you adjust?

3. Have you changed (or tried to change) Thai employees and/or the subsidiary's work practice? If so, what have you changed (tried to change)? What led to the need for change? How did you go about changing it? What were the challenges?

www.ingramcontent.com/pod-product-compliance
Lightning Source LLC
Chambersburg PA
CBHW071209220526
45468CB00002B/554